INTRODUCTION

When I first thought about this project, it was not my intention to rewrite the history of Dawson Creek. I thought I would write down my memories of growing up in the Peace River country, specifically the time period from 1950 and 1960.

I thought it would be a more comprehensive story if it included the reflections of others who share my passion for Dawson Creek. I did manage (with the help of Julie)) to recruit a number of people who shared their stories. I thank them for that.

As my writing progressed, I realized that some history would be necessary to give a complete picture of the city's personality, ruggedness and beauty leading into the 50's and 60's. Thus I have included a bit about the creation of Dawson Creek to set the stage for growing up in this fine city.

I hope you enjoy reading about this journey as much as I have had recalling and writing about it.

Len Ashlee

Acknowledgments

I would like to thank the following people for their contributions and permission to use their stories in this book:

Julie (McGowan) Skead
Judy (Moore) Logan
Roger Fox
Irene (Moffatt) DeBoni
Don Pavlis
Donna (Field) McLeod
Lance Dowd
Keith Skead
Mike Blore
Bill McGowan
Dyanne (Kortmeyer) Johnson
Gail (Walters) Rasmusen
Dorothy McGowan
Errol Erickson
Bruce Haralson
Tom Gannon
Blaine Nicholson
Susan Wood Jensen
Marilyn Hunter Gannon
Brian Fiddler
Bryan Chamberlain

A very special thanks to Julie for her hard work in research, editing, recruiting and especially her words of encouragement.

I would also like to thank the Peace River Historical Society for the use of quotes and pictures used in this book

Len Ashlee

CONTENTS

Chapter One

WAITING FOR A TRAIN

The first train to arrive in Dawson Creek was on January 15, 1931. It was a steam belching fire-breathing dragon whose whistle could be heard for miles.

I was not present on this occasion, but I do have early memories of the sights and sounds of the steam engines. As the train crossed Eighth Street on a cold winter day, you could hear the steel wheels crushing the snow on the tracks. The sound was of an animal screaming in pain. This is possibly the way it was in 1931.

The people of Dawson Creek were excited about having the train terminus being awarded to their tiny community. Many thought that Rolla or Pouce Coupe would be selected over their tiny hamlet. The actual Village of Dawson Creek was about 2 miles west of the end of tracks. The residents were quick to pack up and move to the new location.

The Northern Alberta Railway purchased a large piece of land on which to build a new station and switching yard. They laid out a grid of streets and lanes, which was the template for future building sites. Local merchants purchased the lots and began to erect the buildings that soon became the core of Dawson Creek.

Northern Alberta Railway Steam Locomotive at Dawson Creek

They assembled five grain elevators (eventually eight in total) on the south side of the tracks; a roundhouse along the north side of the tracks and just a little west of the station. The roundhouse contained a large turntable that was used to turn the engines around. A large dugout was built just south of the tracks between 12th and 13th street along side of Alaska Avenue and south to 102nd Avenue. This was to serve as the reservoir of water for the steam locomotives. This water hole was in use until about 1960, when it was filled in and the site was used to build the new City Hall, Fire Department, and Police Station.

Elevator Row

North Side of Station

The steam locomotives rumbled in weekly until the last steam train left Dawson Creek on May 14, 1960. It was driven by longtime engineer Neil Doherty.

The Station was always a beehive of activity after the trains arrived, unloading passengers and their baggage, hand drawn freight carts piled high with bags and boxes being shuffled into the building for sorting. The lobby was filled with people being greeted by friends and family. In the corner was a large potbelly stove that had been stoked with coal providing welcoming warmth. The ticket seller stood behind an ornate brass grill mounted waist high in a wall, which separated the waiting room from the office. Behind him sat the telegraphers tapping out messages to people throughout the world. Roland and Maurice Hardy from the French speaking community of Falher, Alberta, were the men hired to do this job. Morse Code was a language these men understood. It made no sense to me.

Waiting Room

Allen Elliott was the station agent from 1942 to 1963. His son Jim became a friend through high school. We spent many days in his bedroom listening to radio on his crystal set and going through his collection of various electronics. Jim was a collector of sorts, and he acquired an English sports car from Mike Blore, called a Singer with right hand drive.

We would have parties in the residence whenever his parents went out of town. He, many others, and I would be doing the same thing, typical teenage treachery.

"First party for me was at Jim Elliott's at the station. I had just met Keith the Fall of 1961. There were records playing....Keith was upstairs talking to Jim about his 2 way radio setup. I sat and smiled sweetly, no confidence at all, recognizing people older than my 16, but I didn't talk. (Can you believe it?) I went in the kitchen. Guys were making Bloody Mary's....tomato juice and beer? I wasn't a drinker....was supposed to be home at midnight. I waited some time for Keith, with a few drinks under his belt, to get around to driving me. I considered walking home on my own but thought better of it. Keeping my fingers crossed helped me get home safely. I felt like something of interest had happened in my weekend....could tell about it at school! I wanted a life other than school, Girl Guides, going to a 'show' with girl friends, the odd pajama party, part time job at The Hudson's Bay. I grabbed on to it."

Julie McGowan-Skead

Much before the days of partying, my friends and I were fascinated by the grain elevators. We were aware of nothing else as large or awe inspiring. The challenge now was to explore these mammoth structures to the fullest. A look inside was in order. The first observation was the farm trucks, loaded with grain, driving over a slightly elevated steel grate to unload into a pit below. The grain was then augured into the main structure of the elevator. My first look inside was kind of scary. The walls went up forever with large beams holding the structure together. There was a small rope driven elevator that was used to ascend to the top. There was also a wooden ladder built on to the wall. We didn't know how to operate the hand elevator so up the ladder we went. The place was full of grain dust on every surface and in the air...not so healthy for the lungs. We managed to climb to the peak, never looking down. We were very impressed with the structure and the amount of grain it held.

We were also excited about the number of pigeons that lived in the rafters. "Wonder what it would take to catch a few and train them to be homing pigeons?" We did succeed at capturing some, but had no luck in training them. In the end we had to let them go. As it turns out, they were already trained as homing pigeons; they flew straight back to their home in the rafters of the grain elevators.

Built in between two of the elevators, was a stock yard. It was used to hold cattle and pigs to be loaded on the train and shipped to markets in the south. I was not impressed by the inhumane way the animals were treated or the smell of the place. I didn't spend a lot of time there.

The roundhouse was an interesting place. I would go to the large open doors at the time when they would be turning a locomotive engine around. It would drive in on the tracked turntable and it would slowly begin turning the engine around. Once turned it would drive out on the same tracks it came in on; the engines were now facing east and could now hookup with many boxcars loaded with grain.

One day I came upon a steam engine sitting idling at the station. I climbed up the ladder into the engine. There was no one inside, time to take a look at this monster; a seat for the engineer on the right, a large brass throttle lever mounted horizontally reachable by his left hand, a lever on the right for reversing, big brass gauges for measuring steam pressure, a large firebox door which opened into the boiler, a water tender and a coal bin to the rear. The beast just sat there making grunting sounds and dispersing small blasts of steam from various outlets. This thing could eat you alive, time to move on!

After leaving high school I secured a position with the Express Department of the NAR. My job was to unload the express car with mail, luggage and packages. These items we loaded on an express wagon pulled by hand. Once unloaded they were sorted and stored in the shed which was attached to the main station. I was given the waybills that accompanied the express. Customers would come to the station to pick up their goods. The express employee on the train was a total character. He would get off the train and head down to the Co-Op store a couple of blocks away and purchase Margarine by the case. He was purchasing this for customers back in Edmonton. Alberta had a ban on coloured margarine at that time. This was to protect their butter sales.

He had a warped sense of humour as well; On one occasion I was in the midst of loading freight, I became aware of a loud snarling sound from the car. I asked him what in the heck was making the noise. He told me there was a crated bobcat. He pushed the crate towards the door warning me to be careful of its claws. On closer inspection I realized it was some sort of cat. It turned out to be a Siamese Cat. Never having seen one I was indeed relieved that it was just a house cat.

On the train was a conductor as well as a chap labeled as the Newsy. He would go through the passenger car selling newspapers, bottled pop, candy, and chips. He must have had his own private stock of Wobbly Pop. He would get off the train swaying to and fro as though he was still on the train in motion.

One of our close friends owned a Mercury Turnpike Cruiser. This car made excellent transportation when we launched it on the railroad tracks. This car came with 900X15 wheels and when ten to fifteen pounds of air was released from the tires, it fit comfortably on the tracks. With a manual throttle control it could be set to cruise at around thirty miles per hour and remain on the rails. The occupants inside would sit back enjoy some liquid refreshments while on autopilot. Of course this mode of transportation could only be enjoyed under the cover of night. I suppose snapping on the headlights at a level crossing had some unnerving effects on folks approaching that crossing. One section of the trips that always gave us concern was crossing the trestle between Dawson and Pouce Coupe.

We only experienced one problem with riding the rails. In the centre of town we became derailed. We had the advantage of it being in the middle of the night and under the cover of the elevators. In a desperate move we managed to jack up the car to remove it from the tracks. This would have been hard to explain to the railroad officials or the local police department.

Keith Skead

Chapter Two

NORTH TO ALASKA

Yesterday, Dec. 7, 1941, a date which will live in infamy, the United States of America was suddenly and deliberately attacked by naval and air forces of the Empire of Japan.

The first line of President Franklin D Roosevelt's speech which was broadcast to the American Public on December 8 1941. At the conclusion of this speech the US declares war on Japan.

Not many, if any of the 500 or so citizens of Dawson Creek, B.C., realized the impact this declaration would have on them. The fear of a Japanese attack on the Pacific coast, specifically on Alaska, prompted the need for an overland supply route to Alaska. On February 6, 1942 the construction of the Alaska Highway was approved by the United States Army and the project received the authorization from the US Congress and Roosevelt to proceed five days later.

There are many books and publications written about the construction of the Alaska Highway, the facts are for the most part accurate and are indisputable. The stories reflect the harsh and unfriendly conditions that thousands of men faced during its construction. The official start of construction took place on March 8, 1942 after hundreds of pieces of construction equipment and thousands of US troops were moved on trains by the Northern Alberta Railway to the northeastern part of British Columbia at Dawson Creek. Construction began in earnest as the winter weather faded away and crews were able to work from both the northern and southern ends; they were spurred on after reports of the Japanese attack on the Aleutian Islands.

The needs of war dictated the final route, intended to link the airfields of the Northwest Staging Route that conveyed lend-lease aircraft from the United States to the Soviet Union. Thus the long route over difficult terrain was chosen. In 1942, the US Army Corps of Engineers assigned more than 10,000 men, about a third were black soldiers, members of three newly formed "Negro regiments". The US Government also employed approximately 15,000 Canadian and American civilians to aid in this project. There were four main thrusts in building the route: southeast from Delta Junction, Alaska toward a linkup at Beaver Creek, Yukon; north then west from Dawson Creek. An advance group started from Fort Nelson, BC; as well as construction both east and west from Whitehorse, Yukon. The US Army Corps of Engineers received their supplies in the northern section via the White Pass and Yukon Route railway out of Skagway, Alaska.

On September 24, 1942 crews from both directions met at Mile 588 at Contact Creek, at the British Columbia-Yukon border at the 60th parallel; the entire route was completed October 28, 1942 with the northern linkup at Mile 1202, Beaver Creek. The highway was dedicated on November 20, 1942 at Soldier's Summit on Kluane Lake. The highway was not usable by general vehicles until 1943. Even then there were many steep grades, a poor surface, switchbacks to climb and descend hills, and few guardrails. The Canadian portion of the highway from Dawson Creek to the Alaska border, was officially turned over to the Canadian Government in April of 1946 and was opened to general traffic in 1947. The maintenance and upgrading of the highway was placed in the hands of the Canadian Army Engineers until 1964 when it was then replaced by the Department of Public Works.

The Arduous Task Begins

The following is an excerpt from the *Calverley* collection by Day Roberts:

"The face of Dawson Creek changed, almost overnight, with the arrival of 94 members of the US Army Quartermasters Corp on Monday morning March 9. 1942. The troops arrived by Northern Alberta Railway train, in the wee hours of the morning, and were the vanguard of approximately 3000 US Army Engineers, starting the "friendly invasion" to build the Alaska Highway from Dawson Creek to Fairbanks. Dawson Creek's population at the time was about 500 residents, which jumped to more than 3,000 in a very short time. Friendly residents, hitching posts, wooden sidewalks, outhouses, and horse-drawn water delivery greeted those first troops. And of course, lots and lots of gumbo mud, as the heavy increase in traffic churned up the streets. Tent camps sprang up overnight; north of the N.A.R. Station, along the hill north of town, (later to become known as the Loran Station) and on George Chamberlain's property west of what is now 17th Street. Some of the preparations or the arrival of the troops had been carried out in advance, as army officials had earlier conferred in Dawson Greek, and on February 20th approval had been given to proceed with the preparations. The E.J. Spinney Construction Company was contracted to build six huge storage platforms west along what was later to become Alaska Avenue, for the US Army Quartermasters and Marshall Miller had been given a contract to provide ice for refrigeration storage. Quartermaster staff headquarters were established in the three storey building, formerly the "Five to a Dollar Store" owned by Harry Brown. Truckers were waiting in readiness, hotel-men were considering enlarging their premises, and the Carlsonia Theatre began showing movies on a six-day a week basis. The Northern Alberta Railway yards in Dawson Creek were expanded and extended northwest of 17th Street to what became known as the "US Army Railhead Camp." The "Railhead Camp" extended northwest past the present golf course and north along 17th Street to what is now the Access road on property formerly owned by George Dudley. Water and sewer lines were installed and streets were laid out, gravelled and named. US Army Engineer barracks and warehouses covered the railhead camp area. In the days, weeks and months that followed, trainload after trainload of soldiers, construction workers and equipment arrived over the N.A.R. to the bustling railhead town."

US Soldiers arriving by train in Dawson Creek and setting up their tent camp.

The completion and subsequent opening of the highway to the general public in 1947, provided opportunities for fledgling entrepreneurs; the need to distribute supplies to communities along the new highway gave birth to many new trucking companies. Among the first was E J Spinney Trucking; Wilson Freightways (Gordon Wilson); later to join forces with Northern Freightways (Roger Forsythe); Nelson Transport (Warren Nelson) put down roots as well; Trail Transport (Archie Trail), later to lend his name to Rempel Transport to become Rempel Trail Transportation (John Rempel); Calder Transport (Gordon Calder); as well as Loiselle Transport (Paul Loiselle.) These and a few others, constructed warehouses and provided employment for many locals.

Rempel Trail Transport

Aside from trucking companies, the village saw growth in the hotel and motel industry. Many cafe's and restaurants, hardware stores, pool halls and various entertainment facilities sprang up to fulfill the needs of this rapidly growing community. It was rumoured that the US Army found unique ways of disposing of their assets after the highway was completed. One story that was floating around in the 50's, was that a few construction companies got their start in Dawson Creek by digging up bulldozers and earth moving equipment that the US Army had buried in the woods to save the expense of moving equipment back to the US. I don't know if any of this is true, but Mark Twain once said that he would not let the truth stand in the way of a good story.

Driving the Alaska Highway in the beginning was an adventure that was not to be taken on by the faint-of-heart.

The following is from a 1950 publication of the Alaska Highway Travel Guide by the American Automobile Association:

Driving the Alaska Highway

The Alaska Highway starts at Dawson Creek, B.C. It's total length is 1527 miles, of which 1221 miles are in Canada and 306 are in Alaska. The road has a gravelled all-weather surface from Dawson Creek to the Yukon-Alaska boundary. The paved-road driver will find that he must take it a good bit slower on gravel surface until he is used to the roll of the gravel under the wheels Some of the curves on the highway are quite tricky and not all the curves are super-elevated. Braking must be smooth, and every effort and attention turned toward avoiding sudden starts and stops. The greatest length of the highway can be driven at a comfortable 45 miles per hour.

Car Equipment and Service

Travellers cannot expect assistance in matters of food and shelter nor of automotive repairs from the highway maintenance camps. Service offered by repair stations is sufficient for the driver operating good equipment. The following is considered necessary for all vehicles: two mounted spare tires and tubes, spark plugs, fan belt, light fuses, tire gauge, car tools, tire pump, tow rope or cable and a first-aid kit. A spare 5-gallon can of gas will serve to supply peace of mind. For winter driving automobiles must be prepared for extreme cold weather operation. Vehicles should be in good operating condition and be equipped with anti-freeze, rear wheel chains, heater, defroster and radiator grille covers. Winterizing with light oils and greases is necessary, and the use of a fuel additive to prevent frost and ice in the fuel system is recommended. Travellers should be equipped with sufficient heavy winter clothing and foot gear to protect them from the weather in case of breakdown, stall or accident.

Accommodations on the Highway

DAWSON CREEK, B.C.
Dawson Hotel. 54 rooms, 8 baths. Single $2 to $5, double $3 to $7.50. Modern.

MILE 49 - FORT ST. JOHN. B.C.
Condill Hotel, 35 rooms, 6 baths. Single $2 to $3.50, double $3 to $5.50. Comfortable, well kept.

MILE 233
Lum and Abner, 9 units, 2 baths. Double $4 to $5. Plain.

MILE 300
Fort Nelson Hotel, 40 rooms, 6 baths. Single $1.25 to $3, double $3 to $5.50.

MILE 392 - SUMMIT LAKE, B.C.
The Summit. acc. 21. Double $3 to $4. Very plain rooms.

MILE 397
Rocky Mountain Auto Court. 8 units, 2 baths. Double $3.50 to $4.50. Neat, modest rooms; good wholesome food.

MILE 463 - MUNCHO LAKE, B.C.
Muncho Lake Lodge, 12 units, 2 baths. Double $2.50 to $4.

MILE 620 LOWER POST. B.C.
Liard Lodge. 25 rooms. 8 baths. Single $2 to $2.50, double $1. Meals 7 a.m. to 10 p.m.

MILE 710 - RANCHERIA, Y.T.
Rancheria, Hotel, 13 rooms, 4 baths. Single $1.25 to $2.50, double $3 to $4.
Very plain rooms but a better than average meal stop for this area.

MILE 804.5 - TESLIN, Y.T.
Nisutlin Bay Lodge, 8 rooms, 3 baths. Single $5, double $7.50. Unusually nice.

MILE 843
Silver Dollar Lodge 8 rooms. 2 showers. Single $1.50, double $3.

MILE 888 - MARSH LAKE, Y.T.
Marsh Lake Lodge, 8 rooms, 2 baths. Single $3, double $6 to $7. One of the nicer rustic log lodges.

MILE 918 - WHITEHORSE, Y.T.
Regina Hotel. 30 rooms, 4 baths. Single $2.50, double $3.50 to $5. Very plain but well kept.

Lum and Abner's

Fireside Lodge

Marsh Lake Lodge

Watson Lake Hotel

MILE 1016 - HAINES JUNCTION, Y.T.
Dezadeash Camp, 34 mi. s.w. on Haines Cutoff. 15 rooms, 4 baths. Single $2 to $4. Open June 1 to Nov. 1. Adequate.

MILE 1022
Mackintosh Trading Post, 7 rooms, 1 bath. Single $1.75 to $2.25, double$3.25 to $4. Modest.

MILE 1093 - BURWASH LANDING, Y.T.
Kluane Inn, 19 rooms, 4 showers. Single $2.50, double $4.50. Rustic, very comfortable.

MILE 1184
Dry Creek Lodge, 18 rooms, 2 showers. Single $1.50, double $3. Adequate over night stop. Food is extremely plain but good enough.

As one can see in the above accommodations listing, the destinations were referred to by the distance in miles from Dawson Creek. (Dawson Creek being mile zero). The highway crews had measured and installed milepost markers at every mile on the total length of the road. They also added crosses to every place where someone was killed in a car accident, stating the number of people who perished and the date of the accident.

These markers were intended to serve as a warning to people to drive with caution and heed the misfortune of those who did not make it. They certainly had an impact on me; sent shivers down my spine every time we passed one. I have driven this highway many times and remember the dust, mud and snow we encountered along the way. I think the winter was the nicest time of year to drive the road as it was in much better condition. I can still remember the stretch of road between Trutch Mountain (mile 200) and Fort Nelson (mile 300) having so many corners and curves, many of which you could see across the muskeg to the road on the other side.

North of Trutch Mountain

Steamboat Mountain

"Winding in and winding out, leaves my mind in serious doubt,
as to whether the lout who built this route,
was going to Hell or coming out."
(author unknown)

*The following is an excerpt from the **Calverley** collection:*

> In 1946 a post four feet high which marked the beginning of the newly constructed Alaska Highway in Dawson Creek was hit by a car and broken. The post was situated at the corner of 8th Street and Alaska Avenue in the city and was the same as those posts which marked every mile throughout the length of the highway. Jaycees in the city noted the damage and took it upon themselves to have it corrected. The job was passed on to one of their members who happened to be a sign painter by trade,
> Mr. Ellis Gislason.
> Jaycees at that time were well aware of the future impact the highway would have on this city and Ellis saw the chance to draw more attention to the fact. He proposed an elaborate post to be placed in the city's centre. He designed and constructed it out of wood. "Mind you, we never had any idea how well it would catch on", he says.
> On Christmas day 1946, the 10-foot-high post was presented to the city and was placed at the corner of 102nd Avenue and 10th Street. It wasn't geographically the exact beginning of the highway but it did mark the center of the city.
> There was possibly some psychology used in placing the post as well. It was to become the traditional place for tourists to have their picture taken before embarking on the world famous Alaska Highway. This brought them into the city's center.

The original post was slightly smaller than the one which is presently secured to the pavement. "The one I built was only about 10 feet tall, but it was almost exactly the same in design," he says.

"It wasn't fastened permanently either and on Halloween kids used to steal it… they even put hay on it and tried to burn it once," he recalls. One Halloween the post had been loaded into a truck and replaced with a wooden privy. It [the milepost] was later found hidden under the Pouce Coupe bridge. When the post was replaced with a metal one in the early 1960's it was permanently fastened to the spot.

Shortly after the post was originally erected, the Canadian president of the Jaycees visited the city and Ellis constructed a miniature replica as a memento of the city. Although he didn't then realize it, this was the beginning of a lifetime career for him.

The idea of presenting mileposts to dignitaries visiting the city was quickly picked up by the village commission and most other civic organizations. Constructing the replicas started taking up more and more of Ellis's time.

When the miniature posts started retailing in the stores for tourists he developed systems for mass production. His wife, Johanna, helps in assembling and he now buys his materials in bulk.

New sizes and styles were developed. The smallest is seven and one-half inches high and they are worked into convenient desk pen sets, trophies and mementos. Sporting clubs use them for awards, tourists purchase then and very few VIP's get out of the city without at least one given from a civic group.

Ellis is proud of the fact that they are constructed almost entirely of local material. In the summer he and his wife spend Sundays collecting suitable wood and rocks. They polish the rocks and process the wood themselves.

Although another firm in the city has them imported from Japan they are not as well received by the public as the home made ones of Mr. and Mrs. Gislason.

"We make thousands a year," says Ellis, and he estimates that during the past 30 years they have manufactured more than 75,000 of them. "I guess they're all over the world by now," he says.

He estimates that he averages about 50 cents profit on each one which doesn't make for a very lucrative business.

"I use it to fill in slack periods in my sign painting and you know how it is . . . when you start something you want to stay with it." says Ellis.

The Famous Mile "o" Post

My earliest memories of the highway was of trips taken with my parents. The road was very challenging to drive; dust and flying rocks from passing trucks scared the hell out of me as my dad would slow and sometimes stop to wait for his vision to be restored as the dust settled. On occasion the loud bang and shattering glass would startle us as a very large rock would put a very nasty break in the windshield. Other times when it was raining, the road became a soupy mess of mud which would completely cover the windshield went blasted up from on coming traffic. Windshield washers were an option on early 50's cars and to spray water required pressing on a bulb mounted on the floor; it seemed like it took forever to spay enough water to clean the streaking mud off of the glass... one more nail-biting time hoping not to drive off the road. The rough and pothole filled roadway created havoc on the suspension and tires of the car and made the ride for passengers very uncomfortable. It was and adventure I will never forget and at the end of the trip we would all exit the car shaking off the dust which had seeped in through the various seams and cracks in the car.

Driving north from Dawson Creek, the first unusual site was the Kiskatinaw bridge. It was a wooden bridge that was curved to accommodate the approaches. It must have been a feat to built back in the forty's. It still stands today as a tourist attraction off the highway which has bypassed it. One of my favourite stops along the highway was on the south side of the Peace River bridge; It was here that in the late summer that we would make trips to stock up on a feed of corn that could only be grown in this area. It was a true delight to sit down and make a meal of this sweet and tasty vegetable.

Peace River Bridge as it looked in 1943

Peace River Bridge after it collapsed in 1957

The beautiful suspension bridge over the Peace River is one of two that were constructed on the highway, the other is over the Liard river. The Peace River bridge was constructed in 1943 and collapsed in 1957. The journey from Ft St john to Blueberry (now called Wonowon which is in reference to its mileage of 101 on the highway) is unspectacular. The trip from Blueberry to Ft Nelson is much more scenic and would take us up and over Trutch mountain with a view of the Prophet river valleys with the Rocky mountains in the distance. The highway today departs from this high road in favour of the straighter route following the Prophet river.

Liard River Bridge

Toad River Lodge and Flight Strip

From Ft Nelson the scenery changed dramatically when climbing Steamboat Mountain to Summit Lake. The mountain and valley views are beautiful. After following the Racing River for a short distance the Toad River appears in the windshield; it has a roadside lodge with an airstrip right next to the highway. In later years I have landed my airplane here to get out and stretch my legs and walk across the highway to the lodge to have a cup of coffee. The Toad River valley and surrounding area was the guiding area of the Callison outfitters, who spent many years here guiding big game hunters. Following the Toad River west for many miles we soon depart this valley and turn north toward Muncho Lake.

Muncho Lake is a pristine body of water along which the Alaska Highway winds. Along this stretch of road you are likely to encounter Stone sheep standing on or alongside the right-of-way. The crystal clear waters of this lake and the surrounding mountains are breathtaking. Following the Trout River through the mountains and out of the Rockies, we are soon at where the Trout River empty's into the Liard River, one of the largest rivers in Canada. This river flows into the MacKenzie River at Ft Simpson, then on to the Arctic.

Muncho Lake

Liard River

Once across the Liard river suspension bridge, it is a short drive to the Liard Hot Springs which is equipped with bath houses and a number of hot spring pools in which to soak away your weary travelling aches and pains. Following the Liard river north is a seemingly long trip to Lower Post B.C.. By the time we reached Watson Lake Y.T., we have crossed the 60th parallel a number of times before finally staying in the Yukon for about a 100 miles before entering B.C. once again just south of Swift River. Before reaching Watson Lake we passed by the historical sites of Coal River and Fireside and the famous Contact Creek where the southern road builders met those from the north at mile 590.

Liard Hot Springs Lodge

Watson Lake is the site of the famous Sign Post Forest; Originally erected by a homesick soldier and a few others in 1942, it consisted of about a dozen signs with arrows pointing out the distances to their home towns. Today there are close to 100,000 signs of all description and it takes the good part of a day to walk through the couple of acres to see them all.

Watson Lake Signpost Forest

The highway flattens out on past Rancheria at mile 710 then at Swift River we dip back into B.C. until we reach Morley River at mile 752 then back into the Yukon. Teslin Lake is next up, on of the largest lakes in the north, of which a large part is in BC. On to Johnson's Crossing at the north end of the lake. The next point of interest is Jake's Corner where the junction to the Tagish highway and the road to Atlin are located.

Johnson's Crossing Lodge

Johnson's Crossing Bridge

Whitehorse is at historical mile post 918. Whitehorse's history goes back to the turn of the twentieth century when gold was discovered in Dawson City in 1896. The city is built on the banks of the Yukon River and was one of the major staging area during the construction of the Alaska Highway. Whitehorse has a very colourful history and by itself would fill the text of a good book.

Driving north from Whitehorse to Haines Junction, mile 1016, we pass the turnoff to Aishihik Lake. It is on the Aishihik river where the scene of Otter Falls was captured and used on the back of the five dollar bill for many years. I have stood and fished for Arctic Grayling on the very spot. A choice could be made about the direction one could go at Haines Junction; North to Alaska (Fairbanks) or south to Alaska (Haines). We turned north and entered the Kluane National Park which is home to the St Elias Mountain range....the largest mountains in North America are in this range. (Mt McKinley in US and Mt Logan in Canada) The journey along the shores of Kluane Lake is breathtaking; Dall sheep can be seen on the mountains almost anywhere along the lake, but there seems to be a large concentration on the south end. At milepost 1083 is the location of Destruction Bay Lodge, a stop on the shores of Kluane Lake which was owned and operated by my very good friends Hank and Doreen Pirillo.

Entrance to Kluane Park

Destruction Bay Lodge in the 60's

Kluane Lake

The balance of the trip to Fairbanks is a long and arduous journey, which is filled with much of the same amazing scenery that is prevalent throughout the Yukon and northern BC.

In the early years, before the highway was paved, there has been many stories told by those who had driven the route. The truckers would tell of their encounters with Steamboat Mountain, Suicide hill, and many other treacherous hills and curves. Having to put on chains in the winter to make it up these hills; coming down was as challenging as going up. Many trucks and cars would end up in the ditch after sliding on a muddy or snow covered corner.

Driving the highway in the 50's was rewarding as well as challenging; the scenery was breathtaking. Every mile would give a new perspective of the wilderness and the wild life that flourished in the forests and streams along it's 1500 miles. There were many roadhouses along the way which provided a welcoming break from the often tiring drive. One could have a cup of coffee, a home made meal and pastries as well as refuel your gas tank. These stops were conveniently spaced about 100-200 miles apart.

In July on 2011, We made another trip to Whitehorse, Dawson City, Skagway and Haines Alaska in the comfort of our 32 foot motor home. This time the highway was paved all the way and was for the most part in relatively good shape.

Destruction Bay Lodge as it Looks Today

This trip was much more relaxing than the ones I had taken in the 50's and 60's. The scenery was just as breathtaking and drive itself was much easier this time. Our first overnight stop was at Fort Nelson then on past Summit Lake, mile 392, on to and past Muncho Lake, mile 463. On this second day we travelled through Lower Post and Watson Lake mile 620, to our next overnight stop at Teslin Lake RV camp by the Teslin River bridge, Mile 804. The next day it was on to Whitehorse, Mile 918; after spending a few days in Whitehorse showing Carol my old haunts from the 60's, we travelled the Klondike Highway to Skagway. We took the Alaska ferry from Skagway to Haines Alaska and spent the night is this quaint little town. The following day we drove the Haines Highway to Haines Junction, Mile 1016 on the Alaska Highway. From Haines Junction we travelled north to Kluane Lake and Destruction Bay, mile 1083. The lodge there was a replica of one that had burned down in the 60's which was owned by my friend Hank Pirillo and his Wife Doreen. To my surprise it was now owned by a friend that I once worked with in the lower mainland 40 years prior. It was my intention to travel over the "Top of the World Highway" from Tok Alaska to Dawson City Yukon, but my friend advised against it because of the reported very poor road conditions. I took his advice and we travelled back to Whitehorse and from there, on to Dawson City; which was equally beautiful and interesting.

Driving the Alaska Highway should be on everyone's bucket list; it's an experience you will never forget.

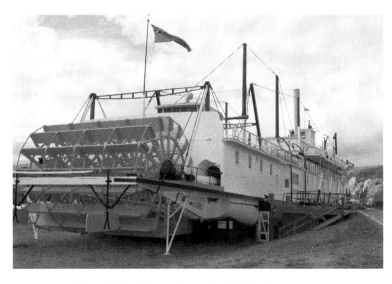

Klondike Riverboat in Whitehorse

Chapter Three

SCHOOL DAYS

The first school I remember attending, was the **Camp School**. (Circa 1947-1952) I think it was a converted army building that was leftover from the construction of the Alaska Highway. It was located east of eight street and south of the road to Rolla. It was an older building that had oiled plank floors, low ceilings and felt more like a barracks than a school. Before class every day, or possibly once a week, assemblies were held in the entrance area to sing the national anthem and say the Lord's Prayer. I do not recall many of the class activities, but I do recall one day at assembly, a girl was standing in the circle as the principal was doing his thing. The next thing we heard was a loud bang; we all looked over and saw this young girl flat on her face in the middle of the circle. She had just had an epileptic seizure. None of us had ever seen anything like this before, scared the hell out of us! I hope she was able to find a way to manage this disorder. I can't imagine her living like that for the rest of her life. My memories of this school are vague as I was only six.

The school I attended next was the **Old Dawson Creek Elementary**. (This school housed grades one to twelve until 1948 when South Peace High School was built.) It was located on the south side of 103rd avenue and 13th street across the street from the Lutheran Church.

Old Elementary School

There was also an annex to the south of the original building, and a new building just to the west. At the south edge of the property, there was a 10ft X 10ft ice house, in the winter someone would cut large blocks of ice and pack them in sawdust. The ice would last most of the summer with water dripping from the cracks in the walls. I never new why they had to have blocks of ice, perhaps it was still used on the trains for refrigeration.

The basement of the Lutheran Church across the street was converted into a classroom. It was my homeroom for a while and my teacher was Dorthea Calverley. She was a very sweet woman, too sweet at times.

One morning she came into class and slammed her books on her desk. The sudden departure from her usually calm demeanour shocked everyone.

She began by saying "It has been brought to my attention that many of the students in this class have been taking advantage of me! Seeking help that was not needed; only to occupy my time and distract me from delivering the lesson for the day." It was true! It was a conspiracy that she did not see happening. I felt sorry for her, but one could not help but admire a group of mischievous youngsters for being able to pull the wool over a teacher's eyes.......no more Mrs. nice guy. We had to work our butts off for the rest of that term!

The new section of this complex had a long hallway with classrooms off to the side. The hallway was used for coats, boots and lunch buckets, as well as a space for kids to play at recess and lunch breaks. One day an enterprising young man, maybe nine or ten, came up with a marble game that captured the minds of most of the boys who owned a bag of marbles.

He had made a board about a foot long and about four inches high. In that board, along the bottom edge, he had cut a series of holes of varying sizes. The object was to shoot one of your own marbles at the board. If it went through one of the holes, you would collect the amount of marbles that was marked over the hole. The size of the hole and the degree of difficulty in putting a marble through it would determine the size of the payout. If you missed, your marble was his.

This soon took on a life of its own; many of the boys came to school the next day with their own board. It was a mad scramble at lunchtime to get a spot in the hallway to set up your own board game.

Teachers who were assigned to lunch detail were supervising this new activity. I even witnessed a teacher admonish a child for making the holes in his board too small. I guess he thought the game was being rigged.

I do not remember how long this went on, but I do recall thinking about it years later and wondered if schools today still condone gambling.

School began at Dawson Elementary (the only elementary school then). I remember the building of new schools in all areas of town to accommodate the post-war baby boom. Talk about large classes! Never heard of teachers complaining about large class sizes, they just brought in more desks and carried on.

Judy Moore-Logan

The **New Dawson Creek Elementary** was built in 1952. My memories of this school are vague. I don't think I even attended classes here. Because of the increase in student enrolment, the old school remained open for a number of years after that.

The New Elementary School

"There was Kindergarten in the basement of Mrs. Edna Tibbett's home on 107th along one side of what would later be Kin Park. Her daughter, Nola played the piano for us to sing along and to play circle singing games. We moved to the new Dawson Creek Elementary School for the last part of Kindergarten in a classroom with a full sized playhouse, a selection of rhythm instruments, a Library corner, counters, sinks, bathroom amenities for our size, our own outside exit, and a milk delivery program. A friend of my dad's, Jim Armstrong from his Ontario childhood town, was a draftsman and finishing carpenter and came to Dawson for the project. That building was 'state of the art'. I wonder where the money came from for our town of around $3500."

Julie McGowan - Skead

"I attended that snazzy new Dawson Creek Elementary School from 1952 to 1958, Grades K to 6. It was along 10th St. near 106th Avenue and was destroyed by fire not long after South Peace Senior Secondary. Once in Grade 4 you could join the band under the direction of Mr. Cuthbert. I secretly wanted to play the drums but it was the trumpet...Dad's....more difficult to play than the similar cornet you could rent from the School District if you had the funds. We mastered, 'Long Long Ago' and 'Little Brown Jug' for starters. I continued in band till end of Grade 9 over at Central Junior High School, under Kurt DeBoer. Thank goodness for Don P. who could read music without starting at C below the staff, letter by letter going up the lines and spaces to get to each note we had to play! Why didn't I practice at home? I had a good memory for playing by ear, so survived, but lacked the confidence to join Dawson Creek's City Band when we were all invited, told there was no band offered in South Peace Senior High School"

Julie McGowan-Skead

"Moving of 700 children to their new home in the $500,000 Dawson Creek Elementary School started on Wednesday of The New Elementary School Built in 1952 last week and is expected to be completed by Tuesday of next week.

The beautiful modern school has eighteen classrooms for kindergarten to grade six. In addition to the classrooms there is a kitchen, an activity room which is a combination gymnasium and auditorium, a multi-purpose room which houses the library, music and is used as a luncheon room, a practical arts room, general offices and the principal's office, store room and medical room. The one-storey section is the primary section and the two-storey wing is the intermediate section of the lovely new school. The classrooms are of the latest design with lots of windows for better light and sloped blackboards, which are green to reduce reflection. Each room is beautifully finished in matching pastel shades and the walls are finished in one of rubbed fir plywood, painted fir plywood, varnished vee-joint or varnished poplar varnished. There were about thirty-two colours used throughout the classrooms, which provide about six different colour combinations. Every classroom has a sink with hot and cold water, a reading room set in the corner with a large bay window and cupboards instead of cloakrooms for the children to hang their clothes. Everything, such as height of desks, chairs, blackboards, and counters is scaled to fit age group to be in that room.

A first for any school in British Columbia and possibly in Canada is the large "picture" or "show" window in each classroom, which overlooks the hallways. These windows are set in the wall and the children can display their work for visitors and other children to see. The kindergarten classroom is self-contained with its own washroom and has a large fireplace, toyland curtains, piano, fishpond, and reading corner. This school was destroyed by arson in May of 1973 and the building that replaced it had none of the outstanding features of the one, which burned."

Excerpt from the files of the South Peace Historical Society

I was looking forward to going to South Peace Senior High; the prospect of being in with the big boys was something I had waited all year for. I was extremely disappointed when I found out that someone decided to take grades seven, eight, and nine classes away from the high school and put them into the newly constructed **Central Junior High School**. I enrolled into grade seven knowing that I would a least be away from the "little" kids!

Junior High School was a time for the teens; pimples, hormones, and Brylcreem. I was not aware of the dramatic changes that were about to happen in my life.

It became increasingly difficult to concentrate on academics, there were too many pretty girls wandering the halls. One of the ways to spend a little more time around them was to enrol in Mrs. Matheson's typing class. Not many boys were in this class.

I actually learned how to type using all ten digits! I didn't know that this skill would be very useful in the future when computers would dominate the world of communications.

Central Junior High School

Mike Blore's father was the Industrial Arts Teacher. His class was fun; learning how to use all the power tools. I made a perfect birdhouse, which I painted blue and green. I was reminded of the adage of the day, "blue and green should never be seen." I didn't care; it looked great to me, perfectly acceptable today! These classes may be why a lot of men have a garage full of tools to this day.

Harry Dewar, the Principal, was a fair man, but was not opposed to dishing out corporal punishment when he deemed it necessary. A few friends and I made the occasional trip to his office for a lashing by his strap. One friend, was in for the second or third time that week. He was particularly annoying to Mr Dewar. He later told me, "from the look on Mr Dewar's face, this punishment was about to be very harsh. He whipped the strap over his shoulder and brought it back down with all the strength he could muster. I could see that this was going to hurt; at the last second, I pulled my hand out of the way. The belt carried on down to Mr Dewar's leg. By the look on his face, I think he hurt himself. I bolted for the door and made my escape." He didn't return for the balance of that term.

TEACHING STAFF AT CENTRAL, 1958 — 1959

Principal - Mr Harry Dewar, Vice Principal Mr. Murray Ryan
Teachers: Mrs. Shirley Wilson, Mrs. Joan Badanic, Mr. Lorne Davidson, Mr. Tom Kerr, Miss Joan Sutton, Miss Roxie York, Miss Maureen Snyder, Miss Rita Kundert, Mr. Dan Calleberg, Mr. Ray Spillers, Mrs. Anne Matheson, Mr. Read, Mr. Schoen, Mrs. McLauglin, Mr. Kurt DeBoer, Miss Frances Mrs. Rogers, Mr. Bill Goddard, Mr Will Durrant, Landon, Mr. Bob McCord, Mr. Peter Blore, Mr. Kerr.

Mrs Anne Matheson   **Harry Dewar**

TEACHING STAFF AT CENTRAL, 1959 — 1960

Principal - Mr Harry Dewar,
Vice Principal - Mr. George Hartford
Teachers: Mr. Walter Schoen, Mr. Jack Wilson, Miss Joan Sutton, Mrs. Shirley Wilson, Miss Roxie York, Miss Maureen Snyder, Mr. Dennis Beaveridge, Mr. Bob Campsall, Miss Rita Kundert, Mr. Peter Blore, Mr. Dowd, Miss Frances Dolan, Mrs. Mabel Rogers, Miss Joan Gray, Mr. Joe Exner, Mr. Ed McGill, Mr. Bob Aitken, Mr. Bill Goddard, Mr Ray Spillers, and Mrs. Anne Matheson

Ray Spillers   **Walter Schoen**

Excerpt from the files of the South Peace Historical Society

Sports were introduced to us in an organized way. I joined the curling club and with many friends, enjoyed participating in this sport at the newly built curling rink.

I was approached by Dale Johnson, and was asked to curl with him in the provincial high school championships. I played second, my cousin Terry Fortin played lead and Lori Ross played third. We managed to win our way to the Alberta district finals in Grande Prairie. Alas, the Alberta finals were not to be, we bowed out there. It was fun to curl in such a competitive event.

The school had a gymnasium that was the home of many sports activities. There was basketball, volleyball, badminton and a variety of athletics. The school produced many teams that one could watch after school and on weekends. It was a great gathering place!

Terry Fortin, Leonard Ashlee, Laurie Ross and Dale Johnson
High School Champs

South Peace Senior High School was for free spirits, cars, and rock and roll. Moreover, we cannot forget higher learning.

"South Peace High School was eventually called South Peace Senior Secondary. We made our own cheer leading outfits under the direction of the Home Economics teacher, Miss Butorac. I remember what I was thinking ..... (Actually, most of my thinking since I was about two). I didn't want to play basketball as I'd surely mess up and cause the team to lose. I figured you were either born an athlete or weren't. I could be connected to the teams, feel a loyal part of my school, travel to Fort St. John, Grande Prairie and Prince George with the teams, be around the cute boys, by being a cheerleader!

I was also elected Girls' House Captain, so got to be involved with the more fun oriented noon hour games of volleyball, floor hockey, badminton and the individual sports in Track and Field.

"There are many stories but a summary of those 3 high school years.....a C to A student after eyes glued to each teacher each lesson, exact note taking, scared not to do homework, scared of all authority, working hard to memorize the right answers, all while fulfilling my need to take in all school functions (organizing some of them), and while waiting for my teenage years to magically include all the romanticism I saw in those 'Archie and Veronica' comic books and those movies with stars like Doris Day, Debbie Reynolds, Sandra Dee!"

Julie McGowan-Skead

"I taught at SPSH starting in 1960. I was appointed in charge of science and math. Ballantyne was principal at the time.

On parents day, when parents came to the school in the evening to meet teachers and listen to what they taught Etc, One teacher, who thought a lot of himself, was talking about his social studies program. Three of us made a sign each. Walked into his classroom and sat in the last row of desks. At the appropriate time we held up our signs for him to see. The signs read "Communist!", "never said that" and "do not believe him."

There was a tall counsellor who limped to his right and a short lady who limped to her left. It was quite a sight to see then both walking side by side, one limping to the right and the other limping to her left!

Then there was the time when the new flag for Canada was being debated. Students took down the school flag, and the flag-pole, held it until dark, then ran up the hill on the road to my house and planted it on my front lawn with their version for the new Canadian flag. It consisted of a beaver holding a maple leaf in its mouth and a frog on its back! The flag made the national news of the day.

I had a master key for the whole school. I did not use it to get into places that were private or out of bounds but just to use the record-player in the main office to record records father made on the piano for the BBC. Ballantyne insisted that I had such a key and wanted it back NOW!! I let him search me all over, desks, home-room, self. But without luck.

I left DC the same year to work in Nigeria. I had 6 keys cut and I sent Gord one every month after I left, with card saying I thought he was a great Principal."

Roger Fox

A note here....re the high school flag pole incident.

"Mr. Fox taught Math and Physics and had the Grade 13 class at SPHS. He would have encouraged Current Events discussions, including the debate over a flag for Canada. I had a Grad party at my house on 96th Avenue in 1964. My dad barbequed hamburgers for whoever dropped in. Seems that night was when the flag pole ended up in Mr. Fox' yard. We saw nor heard any plans. After the incident, Dad's saw.... was returned! I was sure I would be accused as an accomplice!

Julie McGowan-Skead

Murray Ryan Remembers the 1950's

When I graduated from Teacher Training at the University of British Columbia in the spring of 1951, I applied for a teaching position with School District #59 (Peace River South) headquartered in the Village of Dawson Creek. It was the only school district to which I applied for a position, because two years before, my friend, Harry Dewar, had gone north to teach at South Peace High School and he told me when he left Vancouver that if he was still up there in two years it would indicate that he liked it, and for me to come on up. I was interviewed by phone by Walt Hartrick, principal at the time and hired.

Our trip to Dawson Creek from Vancouver was something else again. I had bought a 1937 Plymouth two door sedan, and I did a ring, valve and bearing job on it myself, learning how to do so by reading, asking questions, and renting tools. I asked Imperial Oil for a route that would be easy on an old car, and they sent me down through the States and up through Fernie and hence to Alberta and north. This was, of course, two years before the Hart Highway was punched through Prince George to the Peace country.

We arrived in Dawson Creek on the afternoon of August 8, 1951, in the midst of one of the heaviest rainstorms I have ever seen. The gravel streets in the town were just like rivers. Since there was only a population of 3000 in Dawson Creek at that time, it wasn't long before I found out from someone that Harry Dewar was at the Vogue Theatre with some of his kids. I therefore went there, found him and moved into the house on the corner of 104th and I think about 12th Street, which he was renting from Betty Golata. Fran — Harry's wife —went to England, and we stayed with Harry for the winter, moving the next year into another house owned by Betty.

We were absolutely broke when we arrived in Dawson Creek. However, I quickly learned from other teachers that Art Webb, owner of the Shoprite General Store, was happy to extend credit to teachers who were new in town, so that's how we survived for groceries until I got my first pay cheque. Later that winter we had trouble paying all of the grocery bill one month so I asked Walt Topham, manager of the Bank of Toronto, whom I met on the street, if I could borrow $50 or $75 and pay it back at $10 a month. He replied, "Make up your mind. Which do you want?" When I answered that the $50 would do, he said that he would put it in my account immediately and that I could drop in and sign for it when I got the chance.

When we first went to Dawson Creek, there was not one inch of blacktop in the town. And the mud, even on some of the main streets, was something to behold. There is still a pair of my toe rubbers somewhere in the subterranean mud at the corner of 10th Street and 102nd Avenue. I recall one night walking along 106th Avenue and stepping off the wooden sidewalk into about three feet of water. What a shock that was!

The school year 1957-58 was one of the worst of my teaching career. They were desperate for an English teacher at South Peace, so I lent myself to them for the year, and the board appointed a temporary principal at Pouce Coupe. Unfortunately at Christmas time that temporary principal had some sort of a breakdown and left. The board asked me to principal the school from South Peace, and they appointed a head teacher in Pouce. This arrangement meant that I would spend every one of my spare periods whipping down to Pouce and whipping around the school. I would go down there, see how things were going, perhaps strap a couple of kids, and scream back to Dawson Creek for my next class. When Floyd Irwin, the Inspector of Schools came in to talk to me in my classroom at South Peace it took me a while to figure out about which part of my work he was talking, South Peace or Pouce Coupe. It was a grim and terrible year, and unfair and poor for the pupils and teachers at Pouce.

The first few years I was in Dawson Creek I found that I had to work during the summers to enable us to survive. I worked for the Village of Dawson Creek, mostly on the end of a shovel, along with Harry Dewar. Gordie Ballantyne also drove truck for the village. It was interesting to be working on a sewer installation and talk to my students as they looked down into the muck where I was working. I received $1.00 an hour, and my foreman was Reg Shields. I recall working on the sewer service to the old hospital and running into frost down about 8 feet in the middle of July. We installed water and sewer services by hand in those days, with a crew shoveling out every foot of the trenches in which we then laid the pipes.

I also worked for the School Board during the summers, mostly painting, under the careful guidance of the Maintenance Superintendent, Jack McLaughlin. I told them, when I asked for a job, that I did not want to do bookkeeping or painting. Naturally those two jobs are the ones I did the most.

I will never forget the coldest day that I ever experienced; 62 degrees below zero Fahrenheit. It may have been during the winter of 1956 but I'm not sure. My 1955 Plymouth, a notoriously poor starter in cold weather, actually started that day and I rolled down to the Pouce Coupe Elementary School, where I was principal, on "square" tires. I couldn't get the left door shut because it had been left off the catch all night and the rubber seals were frozen solid so I just couldn't shut it tightly.

Murray Ryan

Excerpt from the files of the South Peace Historical Society

South Peace Senior High School

I was always fascinated by airplanes; I would look to the sky every time I saw a bright yellow Aeronca Chief fly over. (Call sign CF DUK) It was owned by a local electrician who would be flying almost every summer evening. I thought I might like to do that one day.

One day at the airport, while I was drooling over the airplanes parked in the grass by the runway, I came upon a 1940's Cessna 140. It was a beautifully polished aluminum two seater, with two wheels at the front and a tail wheel (Commonly known as a tail dragger.) As I was admiring this great little airplane, I was approached by a short lady with straight grey hair who walked with a pronounced limp. She was accompanied by a man with an arm full of maps and log books. As they got closer I recognized the lady; she was a teacher from the high school.

Miss Steele was the proud owner of this little airplane and she was taking flying lessons from the instructor who was accompanying her. She immediately took on a new persona and along with it, my complete admiration.

She was not a young lady. Even getting into the plane was a bit of a challenge. Undeterred, she threw her cane behind the seat, climbed in and off they went into the wild blue yonder! ...... Hooray for Miss Steele!

Unfortunately this adventure did not last all that long. Sometime later that summer, she ground looped her little airplane and damaged a wing. Tail draggers are notorious for ground looping and are very difficult to land. I think her flying career ended shortly after that mishap.

I was a practising expert on what was expected, the rules at South Peace during my years there: runners, t-shirts never outside of P.E. - no loitering /halls cleared quickly - no business in hallways or bathrooms where you didn't have a class or your locker – notes from home for absence - seating in many classrooms was alphabetical order – only teachers and audio visual club allowed near any equipment - male students couldn't wear jeans, roll up sleeves, untucked shirts, leave even a top button undone - no slacks of any kind allowed by female students or teachers (in Winter, we'd wear them under our dresses and leave them where we passed through the basement open wood box shelving – male teachers wore coats and ties - if getting a ride to school or driving, vehicles, License #, driver's names were registered at office, parent's permission - no hats, jackets, gum, food in class - no slide rules (early calculators) - if you went out while at a dance you didn't get back in.

Julie McGowan-Skead

I asked Julie if she remembered being sent home because she wore a mau mau (loose dress gathered to a yoke) to school. Heaven forbid you might have been taken for being pregnant! Seemed like such a fuss over nothing. Girls are still chastised for what they wear or don't wear. (I guess I am kind of conservative because sometimes I do think they go too far.)

Irene Moffatt-DeBoni

I do remember, but the story went like this. The Bay had gotten in corduroy knee length mau maus, every pastel color one could imagine, for $9.99. All were pretty but I went for purple, as it would be easier to keep clean. I got called to the office by Mr. Ballantyne over the P.A. Very briefly, I was told that a teacher simply thought that other students would be able to look under the loose mau mau as I walked up or down the wide staircase at the end of the hall. If I wanted to wear the mau mau to school anymore I was to wear a belt. A leather belt seemed weird for a mau mau. Purple material wasn't available to buy so I bought black and sewed a tie belt...problem solved! (Of course that made the mau mau shorter so to speak, but no one said anything. Also, do you think the teacher might really have thought it looked like maternity wear and the principal didn't want to use words referring to such an 'unspoken of' state?

Julie McGowan-Skead

I must have been fit, as Central Junior High and South Peace High School were about 2 miles, from our house on 96th and 16th. I often alternated walking and running (usually with 10 lbs. of books) as I would stay in bed till the bitter end. An arrangement for some period of Grade 7 to 12, with Mr. Mel Olsen, Cheri's dad, meant they would pick me up.....If I was ready when he pulled up, which I often wasn't! Being late could mean a detention. Walking.....home a chance for coincidence or fate! I'd watch for cute boys walking or in cars...someone noticing (in the warm months) a pretty dress (which was part of my definition of beautiful), someone to make eye contact with, exchange smiles or a 'Hi' with, someone friendly but not dangerous (What perspective was I coming from?), someone who might ask you to go for a coke or chips and gravy, offer a ride home, ask you to the dance. In a time when it wasn't proper for a girl to phone a boy or even approach one without an excuse, the times for chance encounters were school hallways, at lockers, sitting in the bleachers, lunchtimes, walking home from school, at a show or at the skating rink, at an annual event like the fair, and walking downtown on a Saturday. From the influence of Archie comics and the movies of the day, my ideal life between 13 and 18 needed romantic walks and dates for the shows and dances. Getting a boyfriend depended on one noticing you or, a chance encounter. It was a small and simple world.

Julie McGowan-Skead

Wayne and I were friends since elementary school. We were part of a larger group of guys that formed back in junior high. School was fun for us, I guess, because we were pretty smart and had a nice friendly competition going among us. I guess you might have called us nerds, but I don't think that word had been invented yet. Wayne and I were the only farm boys in the group, though, and I was the only guy that rode a bus to school. Wayne lived in Dawson Creek but his parents had a farm near Rolla.

All of us chose the academic program in grade 9, because we were all capable even though by this time, Wayne and I were thinking of becoming farmers eventually. Whereas the other guys chose electives of the academic type, Wayne and I took all Agriculture electives. Mr. Rose and Mr. Taylor made these classes fun and practical. Wayne and I were the only "nerds" in these elective classes.

By the spring of 1964, foremost in our collective minds was graduation and the anxiety of what was to follow. In our regular classes, students were talking of university and what courses they would choose once they were there. I remember one instance in Mr. Swennumson's English class where we had to choose a topic for a debate. One of the proposals was "What are the important criteria when looking for a marriage partner?" Wow, that was such a foreign idea for me at that time that I was disgusted that that would even be considered. Well, most of the girls wanted to discuss that topic so it was chosen. Anyway, my father was getting old and I was preparing to take over much of the responsibility of running the farm, once I graduated.

During that Spring Break of our grade 12 year, the Future Farmers Club in British Columbia were preparing for a provincial convention to be held in Chilliwack. I, being the president, and Wayne, being the secretary-treasurer of our South Peace chapter were expected to attend. Well, the week before the convention, Wayne and I had a talk and we decided that maybe we didn't really want to go. After all, "We were going to be billeted by some strange farmers." Well, this didn't go over too well with our sponsors, Mr. Rose and Mr. Taylor.

Now here's the outcome of that fateful moment in both our lives that we would never had predicted. Mr. Taylor chose to bribe us to go to this convention by offering to take one afternoon off of our schedule in Chilliwack and drive us into Vancouver and take a tour of the campus at UBC. I think it took Wayne and I about 2 seconds to agree that "billeting with some strange farmers" wasn't that bad after all.

Well, I don't remember too much about the convention itself although we must have spent a few days there. What I do remember is the tour of the campus at UBC. Here we were two naïve farm boys who had never been to the big city and looking at all the facilities that the university had to offer. We were blown away! So back in Dawson Creek in April of 1964, with only a few months before September classes were to start, Wayne and I could not get our applications completed fast enough to apply to UBC. We were both accepted and then a whirlwind of preparations began for our new adventure. Applications for bursaries, scholarships and accommodation were a few of the last minute necessities that had to be handled. What a turnaround from only a couple of weeks prior! I think our heads were in the clouds for quite a while during the last couple of months of our graduating year.

Wayne and I both graduated from UBC; I with a Bachelor of Science in Chemistry and Wayne with a Bachelor of Science in Math. Wayne did go back to farming for a while after graduating. A few years later he looked for new adventures. I never did go back to farming. While I was at university, my parents sold the farm and retired to a small home in Dawson Creek. It wasn't until many years later that I reflected on that quick decision I had made that changed the course of my life. What effect had that decision made on my parents?

My mother was always supportive of a good education and had encouraged me to go. But my dad??? He never showed disappointment, but I wonder if he was hurt by my decision.

Selling the farm to someone outside the family must have been hard for him to do. I never got to ask him that question as an adult.

So a few times during my life, I stop to ponder the questions. What if I had not taken that opportunity? What if I would have stayed on the farm? Do I have any regrets about my decision? Most of the time my answers are the same; I made the right decision……. But it's always fun to think, for a while, about what the alternative might have been.

Don Pavlis

Farming near Dawson Creek

There were a number of schools in Dawson Creek in the 50's and 60's and the one that held the most mystique for me was the **Catholic School**. It was not created by the same governing bodies as all the others; it was founded and supported by the Catholic Church and was staffed by teachers who happened to be nuns. It was well attended by many students from grade 1 through 12.

I don't remember any specific animosity being displayed toward the students of this school, but I sensed a feeling of isolation between these students and those of other schools. I had friends who attended classes there and at times they spoke of the disciplined regiment of combining school and religion. Some had a desire to attend the other high schools simply to be a part of the mainstream majority. In the end I don't think many have any regrets about the education they received from this institution.

Two Sisters of Providence, Sister Louis Omer and Sister Bernice Marie, came to teach at Dawson Creek in September 1944. They boarded at St. Joseph's Hospital and had for their lot 56 pupils Grades 1-8. They began by teaching in the basement of the church. During the year, they bought two surplus American Army buildings which they named Notre Dame School. The next year Notre Dame School opened its doors September 4 to approximately 130 pupils in Grades 1 to 8, fifty of whom were to stay as boarders. To look after these was Sister Yvonne of Jesus, Superior, Principal and teacher, with sister Louis Omer and Sister Angela helping with the teaching, Sister Madeleine as boys' supervisor, Sister Rose Gertrude as girls' supervisor and Sister Agatha as cook. A week later, Sister Ann Clementin opened the Notre Dame Business College with an enrolment of 12 students. They were all amazed at seeing the commercial room well equipped with typewriters and all the standard books usually found in any Business College. On October 22 Sister Jules Octave began teaching music with an enrolment of 35 pupils.

And so, school population increased in the barracks, each year adding another grade to the former until grade 12 was reached. The students engaged in extracurricular activities especially in sports and dramatics. But despite the optimistic spirit of all concerned, each year the old barracks were getting older, and showed their resentment by letting the wind blow in at will, the rain leaking through the roof, and though the furnace kept going full blast the cold crept in. It was then decided to build a new Notre Dame School for the education of the children.

May 22, 1952 marks the blessing and official opening of the new Notre Dame School. In September of the same year, we find 13 Sisters on staff, with 258 students — 63 of whom were boarders — and 20 in the Business College.

Catholic School

Years passed. The city grew. Space needed for classrooms necessitated the closing of the boarding school. No longer able to finance Notre Dame, the Sisters "sold" the school to the parish in 1960. To bolster the diminishing ranks of the Sisters, Bishop O'Grady sent his lay apostles who gave of their time and their talent along with the Sisters, and for the same salary — room and board and a small monthly allowance.

The ways of God are sometimes strange and hard to fathom. The Sisters realized that because the parish still owed the entire debt still outstanding for the school, they would never be allowed to borrow money to construct the church that was so badly needed. The Sisters obtained permission to remit the entire debt and to give Notre Dame Parish the deed to the school. Hardly had the pastor announced these glad tidings to his flock on Easter Sunday, 1968 when in the silence of early dawn, Notre Dame School went up in flames. The Alma Mater which had been the joy and pride of its old students was no more.

Coming to the rescue, the Public School Board offered empty barracks to the parish in lieu of classrooms. And so, after only 16 years, the children of Notre Dame were again in barracks, so reminiscent of the humble beginnings when their parents were students.

Then came the denouement. The parish fell heir to the insurance money at replacement value on the building that had been donated to them just a few weeks earlier. The sum was substantial enough to give them the type of school that would meet today's standards and bear comparison with any of the public schools around them.

And so, on the ashes of old Notre Dame and its hosts of memories, a beautiful new school proudly stands, an edifice worthy of the sacrifices of so many of Mother Gamelin's valiant missionaries who toiled that others might reap so rich a harvest.

Excerpt from the files of the South Peace Historical Society

Chapter Four

THE GOOD OLD HOCKEY GAME

The winter sports were dominated by hockey and curling. The local senior men's hockey team was the Dawson Creek Canucks. They played in a league that included the Grande Prairie Athletics, the Hythe Mustangs, the Fairview Monarchs and the Fort St. John Flyers. The competition was very good, and the players on all teams had a very high level of skill. Some of them had been semi professional and a few had been to the show. The local kids could play with the best of them. The Canucks team was made up of players like: Dave Leoppky, Lloyd Haddon, Paul Roy, Max Swanson, Buster Kyle, Dwayne Bell, Don Switzer, Walt Hanson, Phil Sykes, George Bonner, the Joyal brothers (Frank, Pete and Dave), Ed Diachuck (played in 12 games for the Detroit Red Wings in 1961/62) and, youngsters Jim Kyle, Paul Hanson, and Jerry Lafond. Coach and manager Jerry Thompson contributed to the winning efforts for many years.

I was born in Grande Prairie in 1948 and raised in DC from 1950 to 1965...Spent my youth there. Left in 66 moved to Vancouver to become a Sports Broadcaster and enrolled in the National Institute of Broadcasting. Didn't work out the way I wanted so ended up moving to Edmonton . Met my wife Lise there and never left. Managed a Marine Dealership for the next 8 years. That's where I got into hockey. Started with a group of friends to buy a AJHL team and moved them to ST Albert. Make a long story short I ended up volunteer my time and was the Equipment Manager. Mark Messier was a 15yr old so I got to watch him develop first had. Met a lot of hockey people and started working part time for the Edmonton Oil Kings. Team moved to Great Falls and then Spokane that's where I took over as the Chief scout. The team was folding and the Edmonton Oilers asked me to be the Chief Scout for there junior team in Kamloops the JR Oilers. Was there from 1979 until 1984. Was offered the chief scout job in Pittsburgh, that same year we Drafted Mario Lemieux. One of us went on to own the team, guess which one. After 5 yrs there I moved on to be the chief scout for the Hartford Whalers for 7 yrs 1989 - 96. Then going to the Detroit Red Wings where I have been for the last 20 yrs. Fortunate to have my name on the Holy Grail of Hockey the Stanley Cup. Who would think a boy from DC would have that happen. I still have to pinch myself about that. That's where my story all started in DC growing up playing hockey, watching the Canucks, being a rink rat. I remember those days well. There was a few of my buddies who were like me Eddie Armitage, Ron Millsap, Wayne Weinger, Roger Farrell, Ted & Billy Schields and so many others. We just wanted to play for the Canucks. We used to clean the ice after their games and on weekends would skate all night . The old Arena was like our second home. Also played a lot of hockey on the creek behind my home the Red Bird Auto Court where you could skate for miles depending on the snow build up.

Watching the Joyal brothers was special Frank, Dave and Pete. There younger brother was Eddie who played Pro for the Red Wings, my Dad's favorite team. Amazing after all these years I ended up working for them. He would have been pleased. In later years living in St Albert having two boys and needing a Baby Sitter who do I get but Frank's daughter Mary; strange how life works. Her Dad Frank was my Bantam Coach growing up . Even her mother was my grade 4 teacher. Miss Dick.

Bruce Haralson

1952 Dawson Creek Canucks

Day Roberts gave much of his time for many years refereeing hockey games in this league. It was probably a thankless job! There were a great number of young kids of all ages that made up the many junior hockey teams and leagues. It was a sport that was enjoyed by players and fans alike. The Dawson Creek Memorial Arena hosted many great hockey games. The fans endured through freezing subzero temperatures by stomping their feet to keep themselves warm. "There was no heat in the building in those days" We had public skating on the weekend. The rink was usually full of couples skating to the piped in organ music. We all travelled in a left turning circle around the perimeter of the rink. I could not figure out why I had difficulty turning right when skating on my own.

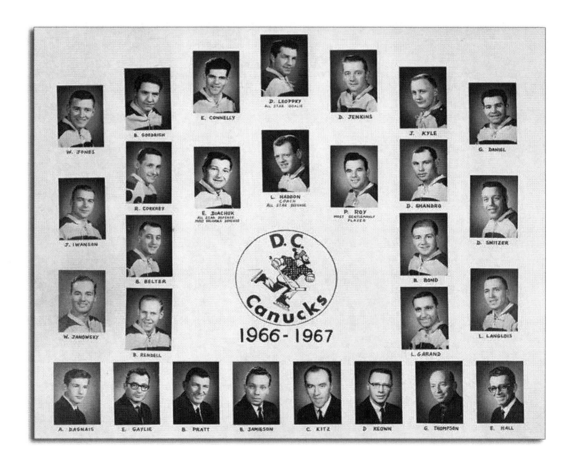

We skated laps to classical music, like 'The Blue Danube Waltz'-Strauss, and Tchaikovsky's 'Dance of the Sugarplum Fairy', 'Waltz of the Flowers', 'Sleeping Beauty Waltz'. As a teen I'd go on my own to the rink and wonder if some cute boy would happen to be there and would offer to tighten my skates! It was said, that a boy wouldn't likely approach a girl if she was in a group! Besides, who would want competition

Julie McGowan-Skead

The original building was destroyed by fire in the early hours of December 24, 1956. It was soon rebuilt and was back in operation by the fall of 1957 alongside a newly constructed 8 sheet curling rink. This building was also the host to many concerts in the summer months. Promoters would bring in many of the current acts that were being played on the radio. It was also a venue for local events; I remember a parade of kids in their Halloween costumes marching around in front of judges who would award prizes for the best dressed. Wrestling was one of the events that came to the city. I was one of the ringside audience booing the participants for their off the wall antics. There were a couple of local men that participated in these events. The highlight of the evening was the tag team midgets. They all put on a great show.

Dawson Creek Memorial Arena

The Dawson Creek Speed Skating Club began in the fall of 1956. Mrs. Pat Underhill arrived in Dawson Creek from Calgary, in September of 1955 and immediately began organization of the sport. After the arena was re-opened, it had been closed for a time to allow installation of artificial ice, Mrs. Underhill made arrangements with Mr. Leoppky, Canucks goalie Dave Leoppky's father, for ice time. Some of the first members were Fay Vandergrift (Clease), Terry Meeres, and Leonard Pever. Archie Field, Bud Geer, and Pat Underhill were the executive until 1960, when official officers were established. Archie Field became President, Bud Geer was treasurer, and Mrs. Underhill was secretary and coach. On December 24, 1956 the arena was gutted by fire and the club was left looking for new ice.

Mr. Underhill built a skating oval at McQueen's Lake, several miles north of town. Mr. McQueen assisted with maintenance duties. The club operated there for a time with their coach also undergoing extensive training for her bid in the World Championships to be held in Finland in 1957. New members arrived at the new oval; Lorna and Gail Scott, Jocelyn Krug, and Sharon Cameron, to name a few.

During their first year of operation the Lion's Club of the city purchased crests for them, but that was their only financial assistance until 1958. With new members appearing steadily a new oval was needed. Bud Geer approached Canadian Freightways for assistance and with their help a new oval was built in 1958. Mr. and Mrs. Underhill, Terry Meeres, and Peter Elmgren built an eight-lap track on the present site of city hall. The Dawson Creek Fire Dept. offered the use of their hoses to flood the track. Later, in the early 1960's, another new oval was built on its present day site behind the arena. Local volunteers also built a dressing room adjacent to the oval. The city took over maintenance duties.

Dawson Creek has a unique position in the organization of speed skating in Western Canada. Red Deer, Alberta is believed to be the first club formed, with Dawson Creek the second and Edmonton third. But Dawson Creek was the founder of the B. C. Speed Skating Association. It was formed in 1956 with Bud Geer as president, making this city the centre of speed skating in B. C. Also, many of the original members here have formed clubs elsewhere. Pat Underhill was involved in Calgary, Mr. Shields set up a club in Esquimalt and Clara and Howard Overend have begun clubs in Mission and Abbotsford. Terry Meeres and Joan Tod moved to Vancouver and began a club there, and Millie Bodnar started one in Fort St. John. Fort St. John was the second member of the B.C.S.S.A. Also, Dawson Creek has produced a number of champions and has had the largest club going. By 1965 there were 127 registered members in the local club. Dawson Creek has hosted the first Canadian Indoor Meet and in 1966 played host to the Canadian Outdoor. In 1964 the club had three Canadian Champions: Gail Scott, Donna McLeod, and Cathy Rome and there have been many outstanding skaters such as Tom Overend, Terry Hadland, Joan Tod and Beverly Bumstead, to mention just a few.

Excerpt from the files of the South Peace Historical Society

We lived in Edmonton before moving to Dawson Creek in 1950. In the early 1950's a lady come into our store and wanted to talk to Archie Field. She, Pat Underhill, spoke to dad about starting a speed skating club here. She had heard Dad had skated in Edmonton (not competitive) and needed some help. She and Dad started the club here. As neither of them had kids that skated they could run the club without influence from other parents. Pat was training for the Olympics (I believe in Norway that year) while she lived in DC. Our arena had recently burned down and Mr. McQueen cleared his "slough" (just north and east of DC) so she could skate there. When the arena was back up and running she would skate at hockey game intermissions against the Canuck hockey players for her training.

Donna Field-McLeod

Speed skating was relatively unheard of in Dawson Creek when Pat Underhill introduced it to the spectators of ice sports. The skates were unlike anything we had ever seen before, long flat narrow edged blades, blunt square ends, that looked like they would be very hard to control on ice. The motion of the skaters legs and arms seemed as though they were hardly putting any effort into the process of skating fast; it appeared like they were not moving fast enough to warrant the title "speed" skating. To convince the skeptics, Pat challenged a very fast player on the Dawson Creek Canucks team to a race. At an intermission between periods of a hockey game, Paul Roy, a speedy forward, came onto the ice and lined up on the blueline with Pat Underhill; the whistle blew and they were off. Paul's feet were moving as fast as they could with short choppy strides, Pat left the line with powerful strides that propelled her into a seemingly effortless motion. As they turned each corner, the distance between them became increasingly greater. Pat crossed the finish line yards ahead of Paul and dispelled any notion of the misuse of the term "speed" skating.

Dawson Creek Speed Skaters

Barbara Ann Scott, 'Canada's Sweetheart' a figure skater from Ontario, had made the 'News of the Day' we got before shows at the movie theatre. She was the 1948 Olympic Champion, European Champion, a two-time World champion, and a four-time Canadian national champion in ladies' singles. (When my sister, Barbara Ann was born I begged my parents to no avail, to name her Barbara Ann Scott McGowan!

Julie McGowan-Skead

I remember when I went to the Ice Capades in our arena. I saw beauty, fitness, costumes, and perfection and wished I could figure skate. I was in Grade 1 and in a large group of school kids asked to be part of a 'half time' sort of thing...we were frogs skating to sit on large paper lily pads (the music was Burl Ives, 'Little White Duck') while older kids did their thing....must have been local figure skaters.

In Grade 1 I fell during public skating at the arena, when a couple of boys zoomed by with a puck and sticks...ended up with a cast on my arm, a broken wrist. St. Joseph's Hospital was run by the Catholic nuns. I remember the ether, and not throwing up after like they expected me to. My REAL figure skates used to be my Aunt Ruth's. She had skated in carnivals with her friend Anna Mae Kitchen! I felt wonderful in them...wore them even as an adult. When I was 12, I ordered a figure skating outfit from Simpson's Sears Catalogue for about $10....black corduroy with pink satin lining....fitted jacket and short circle skirt. Do you think Paul Hanson and others at the Grandview Elementary outdoor ice rink after school believed I was the real thing? I went to an intro freebie but wasn't approached to sign up so assumed my attempts to skate a figure eight and skate backwards didn't show promise. Besides, lessons would have cost money, which I assumed my family (6 children) didn't have the extra for.

Speed skating....remember Terry Meeres? It was a mystery to me how out of the blue there could be kids who could do that. I'd never seen it before. I'd never seen speed skates in a store. There was an outdoor oval behind the arena.

Julie McGowan-Skead

Curling is a sport in which young and old alike could participate. There were leagues available for people of all ages and gender; men, women, junior, and senior curlers. The competition was high level for both men and women. The Dawson Creek curling club had representatives in the Briar play downs. My brother, Walt Ashlee, skippered his teammates Ken Hamilton, third, Murray MacDonald, second, and Chester Lindstrom, lead, to the Alberta finals in the spring of 1961.

Carl Forstad, president of the Dawson Creek Curling Club presents the British Consul trophy symbolic of Peace River Championship to Walt Ashlee, skip of the team which won the P. R. Brier Playdown. Other members of the tea more Ken Hamilton, third; Murray Macdonald, second and Chester Lindstrom, lead. The team is holding Silver Mugs which they won at the Peace River playdown.

A dinner sponsored by the Dawson Creek Curling Club was held in the banquet room of the Curling Rink on Sunday to hail the winners of the Peace River zone Macdonalds Briar Playdown held over the weekend.

Winners of the paydown was the rink skipped by Walt Ashlee with Ken Hamilton as third, Murray MacDonald as second and Chester Lindstrom as lead.

This will be the first time in the history of the Peace River Curling Association that a rink from Dawson Creek has won the right to go to the Championship event. The rink was jubilant over their victory and highly confident of the showing they will make in Edmonton this coming week-end at the Championship event. The Alberta championship will be played off at the Menorah Rink in west end Edmonton.

Jensen Rink In B.C. Bonspiel

The best of B.C.'s Legion curlers meet in the provincial finals at Penticton on February 24th to 26th The finalists will go to the Canadian Legion national finals at Trail on March 14-17.

Representing the Peace River zone in the event is the Gus Jensen rink of Dawson Creek.

In the fifth national Legion event a team from each province will compete for the Gooderham and Worts trophy. Some 7,000 curlers will have taken part in the eliminations at Legion branch, district and provincial levels. Over 680 B.C. Legion curlers take part.

Last year, B.C.'s entry in the national finals was from Nelson. The team was skipped by M. B. Ryalls and included L. W. Bicknell, Roger Hesse and Doug Winlaw.

Date of the Brier itself is not known yet but it will probably be in the first week of March. Scene of the event this year will be Calgary, Alberta.

The playdowns at Peace River were all close scores and competition was keen all the way. Rinks facing the Ashlee foursome were Mel Watchorn, Fairview; Lloyd Larson, Sexsmith, last year's representatives of the Peace River zone and the Fredberg rink of McLennan.

In the A event Ashlee defeated Watchorn 9-6 and went on to take the Larson contingent 8-6 to win the event.

In the B event Ashlee met Larson and won by a score of 6-5 going on the defeat the Watchorn foursome for the second time in a game which was thrilling until the last rock was thrown. Features in the game were three blank ends, a tie coming home which forced an extra end in which Ashlee laid one with his last rock to win the event.

Mr. Carl Farstad, president of the local club did the honors at the dinner for the Peace River Curling Association, presenting Walt and his partners with the British Consols Trophy, symbolic of the winning of the Peace River Championship.

The best wishes of all Dawson Creek go with the four this Friday and Saturday when they travel to Edmonton to play the representatives of Northern Alberta, Southern Alberta and N.W.T. to see who will represent the province in the Brier competition.

The ladies of Dawson Creek were well represented on the national curling scene. My sister-in-law, (Walt's wife) Bernice Ashlee played second on a team that represented Alberta in the Canadian Women's Championship in 1963. Mickey Down skipped this team and the other members were Joanne Bennett, lead and Sheila McKenzie, third. The winning of the Alberta play-downs by this team created a conundrum for the Alberta Curling association; it did not have a team from Alberta representing them in the National finals. There were two teams from BC in the National play-downs. They were quick to rectify this problem the next season by not allowing Dawson Creek to be a part of the Alberta Curling Association. The next season the women had to compete in the BC provincial play-downs. Had my brother's team won the Alberta finals, it would have been the same scenario as with the ladies. Fortunately or unfortunately, which ever way you look at it, this did not happen as Hec Jervais won the Alberta finals that year and went on to become the Canadian champion. Both the Junior and Senior High Schools supported curling and established clubs for students to participate in. We had a lot of fun and enjoyed the competition and comradery.

Curlers are: Joanne Bennett, Bernice Ashlee, Sheila McKenzie and Mickey Down

There were many good players in Dawson Creek's stable of curlers like: Walt Ashlee, Matt Kmet, Chester Lindstrom, Jack Fynn, Gus Jenson, Murray MacDonald, Ken Hamilton, Wayne Tower, Martha Tower, Fay Lindstrom, Micky Downes and many others.

Dawson Creek Curling Rink 1957

I recall Mom being in the odd curling bonspiel as a sub, and my Grandpa Harper curling regularly...often went to watch his games. Jessie Newby was also a regular curler, as well as June Didow. When bonspiel games were broadcast on the radio (mom said they were on the Grande Prairie station,) my mom would use the cardboard dividers from Nabisco Shredded Wheat and draw out the curling ice diagram. She used coloured buttons for the rocks, placing them as the calls were made by the sports announcer.

Julie McGowan-Skead

Summer did not stop the game from happening. Dawson Creek sponsored one of the best midsummer bonspiels in the country. Ice was installed in the curling rink and arena, which by this time had artificial ice. This summer event attracted over sixty teams who curled into the wee hours of the morning to accommodate the full slate of draws. There was always a huge banquet on Saturday night, music and partying was one of the main attractions. Good times were had by all!

Skating on frozen ponds, curling, hockey, hunting and fishing. After the demise of our local arena in a devastating fire we were left with nothing to skate on but our local lakes and ponds. Having emigrating from the Peace River, Alberta area this was the norm. Moving from that area, to Dawson Creek was a real treat to have a covered ice arena.

My father and other volunteers erected a set of boards around the ice surface so that we had a place to skate. This was used until the weather was warm enough to start with construction of a new building.

We played hockey in the new arena but had a lot of fun playing "farm teams" and I mean farm. We, in our fancy uniforms would play against teams that resided in the rural areas. We played in open air rinks and lost more games than we won. Reason; They knew where the pot holes were on their ice surface. We either tripped or lost the puck in these holes. Revenge only happened when they came to play on our new fancy artificial ice and a long distance between goal nets. Our version of a road trip was to make our way to Grand Prairie Alberta, about sixty miles away. Curling was big in town. The first arena only sported a couple of sheets of ice. The season was dictated by weather cold enough to freeze the natural ice in both the curling rink as well as the old arena. Len Ashlee myself and a couple of other fellows joined the curling club in school. Len's older brother was somewhat a pro at the game but I will leave this up to Len to expand on. After curling there was the trek to "Ben's Cafe" to put back some chicken in the mug and rehash the game we just played.

Hunting was a big portion of our lives when in season. Every seventh years the bush rabbits went into a cycle. The became so numerous they dominated just about everything. We would ride on the hood of a car down the back roads and eliminate as many as possible. For those of who are squeamish, let me explain. These critters were diseased and their life expectancy was only a few short weeks. In the winter, the kill rate on the highway between Dawson and Ft. St John became known as the fur lined highway of the North. The side effect of this was broken, frozen bones that raised heck on tires.

In the fall, bird hunting came into play. We spent a lot of time in pursuit of Prairie Chickens, Ruffed grouse and water fowl. A few of our mates did some big game hunting but most were burning up their ammunition on small stuff. For ducks and geese we would take a trip into Alberta where the skies were black with thousands of both species. We went after them like we were using seventy-seven millimeter sky sweepers, like the deck hands on a destroyer used. I think what saved that province from sinking from buckshot, was hunting was not allowed on Sunday.

Keith Skead

Chapter Five

CENTRE FIELD

Spring did not come soon enough for those of us who were involved in Little League baseball. There were enough kids available to field about four teams. We were soon signed up to the various teams and off to the ballpark for spring training and new uniforms. There were many dedicated coaches that gave of their time to instruct us in our endeavour to play the game. This was the thrill of the summer for me. I loved baseball. I played the game into my late teens, playing in pony and junior leagues. The senior men's teams played ball in the fair grounds where the curling rink is now located. I think it was also the grounds of the summer rodeo. Later the senior men's league moved to a newly constructed ballpark on the Pouce Highway across from the drive-in theatre.

I loved to watch the seniors play ball. Plenty of action and a place to pickup a few pointers to take back to the little league field. The chatter from the catcher, Oliver Stewart, was fascinating; the fast and furious banter was intended to put off the batter and to encourage his own team mates. The sound of the baseball as it struck his mitt or the crack of the bat as the ball soared out to the outfield was all part of the sights and sounds of the baseball game.

Norgas Jets Fastball Team 1962
Roy Bell - Ward Averill - Walt Ashlee - Louis McLarty - Bob Barclay
Don Switzer - Bud Hunter - Corky Corrella - Harry Clarke

The game on our field was not as fast paced, but it did have all the elements of a real ball game. There were a few more errors in the field and lot of strikeouts at the plate. We had fun! On one occasion, when I was playing third base, a line drive was hit directly at me. I didn't get my glove up fast enough to catch the ball. It deflected off my glove and straight into my upper lip; lots of blood and a very large lip. This did not deter me; I was back at it the next game with a new readiness in my glove.

I played with a number of kids who shared my passion for the game: Terry Dahlen, Bob Peterson, Lance Dowd, Wayne Constant and Steven Wood, to name a few. We travelled all over the Peace River district, playing ball in tournaments in many communities that sponsored baseball. I don't think we won many of these competitions; it was all for the love of the game!

Harry Dewar's Little League Team

"Little League came to Dawson......I think it was 1955. I tried out and luckily made the team. That meant you got a uniform. I really didn't want to be stuck on the farm team; they just got t-shirts. Our team was the Tigers. There also was the Yankees, Giants and Red Sox. Out coach was a great guy, Bo McIver. Some of my team mates were Greg Vikshus, and I believe Terry Dahlen, Bob Peterson. I played center field the first year.

They were great years. The Red Sox had a very good pitcher....very fast. My knees were shaking every time I got up to bat, but Bo was a very patient coach.

I played ball for about 20 years......loved the game."

Lance Dowd

When I played I was on the Giants, Russell and Roger Farrell, Larry Scherk, George Nolan, Lyle Stearns, Larry Sarich, Kurt Fisher, Wilfred Beaulieu, Verdie Fick, Randy Averill, my brother Bruce among many others. Our coach was Ernie Williams and was a great man. Sometimes as little as 1 or 2 new players made that team. The most was 3 when Verdie, my brother Bruce and I made the team. Actually Alvin West introduced us to the coach and on Alvin's word we were on the team. We won a lot of championships with that team. Mr. Craig and Mr. Dewar coached the Yankees. Bo McIvor still coached the Tigers when I played. Mr. Doherty was coaching a team from the hill. I think it was the Red Sox. My grade 5 teacher coached the Braves and I believe Pouce Coupe Indians were coached by Doyle McNabb.

Brian Fiddler

Dawson Creek had a nice nine-hole golf course that had a strong membership. As a kid I didn't have too much interest in golf. On one occasion, my cousin and I decided to try the game out. We could not afford the green fees so we decided to get up at three in the morning (in late June the sun was up about that time) to get our round in before the course opened. We packed our bag of clubs and balls and off we went to the course. We finished our round just as the clubhouse opened. I don't think we fooled anyone about our presence there as we sat in the clubhouse drinking a pop.

Before bowling alleys had automatic pin setters, I remember having a job setting pins in the old bowling alley next to the Vogue theatre. It was hard work gathering the pins, stepping on a lever that raised metal studs from the floor upon which you centered the pins, then gathering the balls and placing them on the ball return. On a league night it was expected to be done at a blistering pace or suffer the scourge of the bowlers yelling down to "hurry-up". It worked up a sweat for ten cents a line; five players on each team amounted to one dollar for one game. I think there should have been a danger pay clause embedded in the pay structure as there were a few who would throw the ball so hard that the pins would fly from one lane to the next. Ducking these flying pins was hard to do, as you sat in an opening between the two pits, occasionally getting hit in the legs. The scariest of all the bowlers was Ralph Atkinson! His ball would scream down the alley, splattering pins everywhere. Perhaps this is why he was the Canadian Men's Five Pin Bowling Champion. The bowling alley moved to a new location on 102nd ave. across from the Crest theatre. There were high school leagues established here which provided many hours of competition and comradery.

Ralph Atkinson

Chapter Six

NO PARTICULAR PLACE TO GO

Getting a driver's licence was priority number one after your 16th birthday. Written driver exams were studied for like nothing ever studied for in any high school subject. Once a passing grade was accomplished, it was into the car and around town with an examiner to complete the road test portion of the exam; all the time praying not to make too many mistakes or let the examiner see how nervous you were. "Can I borrow the car Dad?" Off to pickup your friends to begin an odyssey which would not end for years. Cruising the streets of Dawson Creek for the first time opened the door to a brand new social environment. The possibilities were endless. The movie "American Graffiti" was a reasonably accurate depiction of the life we were living. I could identify with most of the characters in it. I love that movie! The music from the car radio was the best; Elvis, Buddy Holly, Chuck Berry, and all the great rock and rollers of the day. Rolling down 102nd avenue hanging your arm out the window on a warm summer's evening was the coolest thing to do. Up and down the same streets didn't get boring; it was necessary to find others doing the same thing. There was an occasional pit stop at Wing's Café or Mcbee's drive-in to grab a coke and check for girls who might want to go riding.

Dawson Creek's Main Intersection

My brother had a 1957 Bel Air two door hardtop with a continental kit which was moulded into the rear bumper. It was black and white with a matching interior. It was a gorgeous car that had me pleading with him to let me drive it. One day, in a weak moment he let me go cruising in it. I was soon driving up and down main street hoping that everyone in town would see me in this perfect automobile. I stopped at a red light by the Mile Zero Post and happened to glance in the rear view mirror; behind me, in my father's car, was my brother grinning from ear to ear. I had to pull over and have a chat with him. "What's wrong? Do you not trust me?" He laughed and said he was just checking up on me. He drove away and left me to enjoy an afternoon of extreme pleasure.

The next step was to get your own car. My first was a 1957 Ford Fairlane two door hardtop. It was one of the nicest cars in Dawson Creek, at least I thought so. I had to get cruiser skirts for the rear fender wheel openings, just to add the perfect finishing touch. It had a Thunderbird engine that would smoke the rear tires in a drag race. Of course I had to install "Hollywood" mufflers to make it sound like a really hot car.

This beautiful sound would become one of the targets for the Cops. They would use any excuse to pull me over. One day they gave me a ticket for loud exhaust and allowed three days to get it fixed. I was not very happy about having to put the stock exhaust back on the car.

I decided to stuff steel wool down the pipes and put nails in holes I had drilled in the pipes to keep the wool in. Down to the police station I went to have it inspected. I revved the engine up for the cop to listen to the quiet hissing noise that was now coming from the exhaust. Having passed inspection for the noise complaint, they had no choice but to dismiss the ticket. After driving away from the police station I was now free to pull out the nails and blow out the steel wool. I would be more alert to the presence of the police in the future.

There were a number of teenagers who had their own cars. LeRoy Sandnes had a beautiful blue and white 1956 Ford Crown Victoria. Bob Peterson had a very nice 1958 Chevrolet Impala 2 door hardtop.

Not everyone had beautiful cars, but it didn't matter as long as you had wheels! Pat Kilgour had a 50's Ford with a flat head six cylinder, Keith Skead had a 1953 Chevrolet four door six cylinder, Bill Waters owned a black and white 1955 Pontiac. Terry Gosselin had an older Chevrolet that propelled him around quite nicely. Murray Logan had an early 50's Ford pickup that I helped paint "Magenta". Fred Richter had a 1957 Ford 2 door which he had painted 2 tone blue; he continued to drive this car until well into the 2000's. It was all in the eye of the beholder! Of course Mom and Dad had some cool cars; Chuck Nahumko's mom had a 1958 Edsel Pacer two door hardtop with the transmission selector in the center of the steering wheel. It was a nice shade of pink and white.

"I sent my dad down town to get me some paint for the 51 ford I had done up, said get me some metallic brown; he found coral on sale. That's how I wound up with my first car being a little on the pink side, the girls loved it, me not so much. That's my first car story; I was 16."

Lance Dowd

My first wheels was a 1951 BSA Motorcycle which I bought and re-built shortly after I turned 16. There weren't too many odd balls like myself that rode motorcycles in those days but there was a few of us. I didn't get a car until I was 18 and it was definitely not cool ride.... just a 1956 Dodge 4 door sedan but it did have a V8. One guy who always had nice cars was Mel Hiney. He had a 1956 Dodge (I think it might have been a hard top) with fender skirts so it was much cooler than mine. He later got a 1955 Chev Belair 2 door hard top red body and cream top. Mel used to race stock cars and he won the championship one year. His mechanic was Jim Bacon - I remember all that because I used to date his sister Joy. Of course there was also Fred Richter with his 1957 Ford 2 door hard top and I think it had a lowered back end which seemed to be the style in those days.

Errol Erickson

The weekends were the most exciting times; rarely was anything planned, but there was always something going on. Finding out what and where was as much fun as actually being there. Phone calls, driving from house to house, and stopping friends in cars on the street usually produced the desired results. We were soon off to places like Riley's crossing for a bonfire and wiener roast. Having your best girl cuddled up beside you and meeting up with your friends was the perfect way to spend a Saturday evening. There were times when we all suffered from boredom which led us to explore the surrounding communities. A trip to Fort St. John, exploring the haunts of our rivals, was good for an afternoon of relief. It was always a challenge surviving the unfriendly streets of a rival town. Although we were friendly with a few of our counterparts, the remainder of them did not like us cruising their streets trying to pick-up their girlfriends. After a few close encounters with the locals, we decided it was much more fun to be at home.

I remember the Singer, it was a British car that I had sold to Jim Elliott; he really liked that car. We spent a lot of time in cars when we were teens, gas was cheap and lots of roads. Do you remember you and I having a car race from Ft St John back to Dawson Creek one night? There was a loud bang coming down Kiskatinaw hill and I blew the engine out of my dad's 53 Ford station wagon. You were driving your dad's Ford, a 55 I think. My dad didn't say a word when I told him about the motor, so I thought I was going to get away with it! Riggghhhttt! I spent the next 3 weeks including weekends, at Melnik's machine shop overhauling the car engine. I had a lot more respect for vehicles after that. You were good enough to tow me back to Dawson that night, so thanks again. Then there was Billy Waters with his mom's Desoto; how he lived through those years is beyond me. Two dollars worth of gas was good for an evenings cruising, around town or in the country on weekends. There were dances in all the small community halls around Dawson every weekend. Remember

Chamberlain's pastures? A few parties there. All in all we managed to have fun without doing any damage, never bored and we enjoyed growing up in Dawson Creek. In the middle of summer it never got dark, just a kind of twilight for an hour, then back to daylight by 2 am. Winter was a different story however! It was always nice in the Fall up north, but I wouldn't trade it for the coast having lived here for so many years.

Mike Blore

Mike and I hung out together a lot in our teen years. He had a unique flare for the outrageous and sometimes crazy things things we would do. I recall one day he suggested that we go fishing at Swan Lake, he wanted to try out a spear that he had acquired somehow. We borrowed a boat and motor (I don't know who it belonged to.) and backed up to the trailer with Mike's dad's station wagon, only to find that there was not a hitch on the car. That did not deter us! We propped the hitch tongue onto the rear bumper, wrapped a chain around it and off we went.

As we were approaching Tom's Lake, I looked to my left in time to see the boat and trailer passing us in the ditch. The chain had come undone and the trailer departed from the car. It bounced a few times but stayed upright and did not sustain any damage. We managed to pull it out of the ditch and reconnect it to the car. We arrived at the lake without any further mishap.

After launching the boat, we set out to try Mike's new method of fishing. I was driving the boat and Mike was perched on the bow with his spear in hand and his arm cocked and ready to fling this weapon at some unsuspecting fish. After a couple of unsuccessful tries and Mike retrieving his spear with the rope he had attached to it, the next throw went under the boat. I could see that this had the potential for the rope to come out the back and become entangled with the propeller of the motor. My quick reaction of shutting off the engine prevented this from happening. Unfortunately for Mike the sudden stop propelled him overboard into the lake. He came up out of the water gasping for air and reaching for the side of the boat. Thankfully he knew how to swim! As much as I realized the seriousness of the moment, I had a very hard time suppressing the laughter that was building inside.

Chapter Seven

DOWNTOWN

Leo Zamburec was the owner of "Leo's Shoe Store", which was located on the north side of 102 avenue between 8th and 9th Street. Leo was a very kind man. As well as selling shoes, he dedicated his time to Cubs and Boy Scouts.

I remember going into his store with my mother to be fitted for a new pair of shoes. The fitting process was an experience I remember to this day. Beside the obvious measuring and trying on new shoes, he had a machine that could x-ray your foot inside the shoe. It had three viewing portals, one for the person being x-rayed and, two for observers, presumably for the clerk selling the shoe and an interested parent. We could see the bones in my feet live as I wiggled them around.

I don't know how much radiation I and others absorbed during this process, I can still walk today and I don't think I have any side effects from radiation exposure.

I remember Leo from Leo's shoe store quite well. Not only did he fix all our shoes but he was the bass drum player in the band. Kept us all on beat marching down the street. A really nice guy with a great sense of humour. I remember Brian Kortmeyer and I hanging out at the Dairy Queen one day and wandering over to say hello to Leo. His shop was right next to the newspaper office at that time. Probably also around 1966 Leo thought it would be funny to nail high heels to Brian's shoes. Brian was out walking on the sidewalk in them and we were all laughing. Someone from the newspaper took a picture and it ended up in the paper. Leo was front and centre, always a good promoter.

<u>*Bill McGowan*</u>

Leo's Shoe Store...they were wonderful people... kindness itself. I loved the deep rich smell of the leather. All the different shoes fascinated me...my taste for shoes I guess a part of the forte I was developing for fashion and clothes design.

<u>*Dyanne Kortmeyer-Johnson*</u>

Leo Zamburec

Xray machine

Across the street from Leo's Shoe store was Empire Cleaners that was owned and operated by Jack Holem and his wife. He was the first person, to my knowledge, to own a 1959 Ford Thunderbird in Dawson Creek.

Empire Cleaners and McLevin Brothers

My Dad and Mom had a men's store on 10 Street right next to the CIBC. It was Field's Men Wear. There was a small store separate from but in the same building as Dad's store and it was Lady Fair Shoppe owned by Myrtle Coxe. That was in 1959. Dad had his store from 1950 to 1962. We lived behind our store from 1950-1956. We then moved to 111 Ave near where the "new" hospital was built! Next to our store was another convenience store "Paul's". This was owned by Paul Mah. He also owned Mile Zero Cafe which was next to Kittson's Drug Store on 102 Ave and later moved to 17 Street.

<u>*Donna Field-McLeod*</u>

Radio station CJDC was located on the southwest corner of 102nd avenue and 9th street. This business was owned and operated by the Michaud family. From these studios came the sights and sounds that fostered the social makeup of many living in Dawson Creek. It is too easy to understate the significance this radio station played in the every day lives of the members of our community. It was our ears and eyes to the world around us; almost everyone tuned in to listen to the news every evening at supper time. Eventually we would watch world events unfold via the new medium of television. (The first telecast was aired January 15th 1959.)

The news was followed by The Hospital News....details of who was admitted, who had a baby, who went home, even what was wrong with them.

Radio music broadcasts were separated by genre; Country, Rock, Classical and Gospel were the main formats. I think Country had its place for an hour most afternoons, Rock was predominate on Saturdays, and I think Classical and Gospel shared most Sundays. My listening was mostly to country and rock.

Listening to Hank Williams, Hank Snow, Ernest Tubb, Ray Price, and other members of the "Grand Old Opery", was the first music I was exposed to. Whenever I hear "Your Cheating Heart", "I've Been Everywhere", "City Lights", or any of the great old country tunes played on the radio today, it instantly sends me back to the 50's and 60's and life in Dawson Creek.

Radio Station CJDC in the Late 50's

In the fifty's, we were introduced to Elvis' "Blue Suede Shoes" and his "Hound Dog", soon to be followed by Buddy Holly and "Peggy Sue". Ricky Nelson's "Hello Mary Lou", Tommy Edwards' "Its All In The Game", The Platters, Paul Anka and many others made their contribution's to a great day of listening to CJDC. Hearing this music today, once more transports me back in time.

Before TV, the radio station would also broadcast syndicated shows from major networks in the USA. The sound of the William Tell Overture on Sunday afternoon was the signal for my brother, cousin and I to gather around the radio and listen to "The Lone Ranger" and his partner "Tonto".

"The Shadow" was a scary show to listen to, Lamont Cranston was already invisible to us but our imagination let us believe that we were not the only ones unable to see him. "The Damon Runyon" Theatre was also a source of worthwhile listening. The imagination of children today is not nurtured by the same stimulus as it was in the 50's.

"Faster than a speeding bullet. More powerful than a locomotive. Able to leap tall buildings in a single bound." "Up in the sky! Look! It's a bird! It's a plane! It's Superman!" Opening lines to the Superman Radio Show.

"The Closet, McGee's frequently opening and cacophonous closet, bric-a-brac clattering down and out and, often enough, over McGee's or Molly's heads. I gotta get that closet cleaned out one of these days". Fibber McGee and Molly Radio Show.

Jack Benny was returning home when he was accosted by a mugger. After asking for a match to light a cigarette, the mugger demands, "Don't make a move, this is a stickup. Now, come on. Your money or your life." Benny paused for the longest time, and the studio audience, knowing his skinflint character ,laughed. The robber then repeated his demand: "Look, bud! I said your money or your life!" Benny snapped back, without a break, "I'm thinking it over!" This time, the audience laughed louder and longer than they had during the pause. The Jack Benny Show.

TV.....Well, my family got a 'black and white' TV when I was in Grade 10.....that would be 2 years after 'it' came to Dawson. (There was no credit back then; money had to be saved up!) I remember the Sign out, National Anthem and test pattern coming on at 11 PM. The shows I recall although mostly reruns at the time, are: 'The Friendly Giant', 'The Ed Sullivan Show', 'The Dinah Shore Chevy Show', 'Country Hoedown', with Tommy Hunter and Gordie Tapp, 'The Perry Como Show', The Mickey Mouse Show' (in particular, Annette Funicello...later in movie, 'Beach Party' with Frankie Avalon, and, apparently she and Paul Anka were 'a thing' and he wrote "Puppy Love" and "Put Your Head On My Shoulder" Around that time.

Dawson Creek had its own cooking show, with Cathy Duncan. A friend of ours, Bill Waters, who worked at the station, told us how he and Allen Newby got to eat the food.

Sometimes my mom would do her ironing in front of the TV. Homework had to be done before TV.

Julie McGowan-Skead

I do remember when TV first came to town. We had one of the first, and the neighbourhood kids, many of my brothers' friends, flocked to our house; that was fun. On a Saturday night if we ran home real fast from the theatre we could watch another movie free!

Dyanne Kortmeyer-Johnson

The television studio, which was located in the back of the building, was the source of many great local productions. My friend Bill Waters was the man who captured the action unfolding in front of his camera. Alf Walsh and his Ramblers managed to assemble in this tiny studio, and put on a great country music show featuring the talent of the musicians in his band and the Singing Sweethearts.

A huge part of being a kid in Dawson was being glued to the radio on Saturday mornings to hear our local hero "Uncle Lee" who read stories and ended the show with the most important thing.....reading the names of kids who had a birthday in the last week. They were listed in "The Big Blue Birthday Book" and every kid just had to have their name in it. Thanks to CJDC and "Uncle Lee" for the wonderful memories! I had the bonus of living across the street from the family and am friends with the family to this day.

As a teenager I enjoyed many a dance to the music of the Dynamics and the Nighthawks. I could hardly wait for the weekend for the dances. Sometimes they were above the curling rink but my strongest memories were of the dances at the Sportsman's Hall which overlooked Kin Park and the Soap Box Derby track.

Judy Moore-Logan

Top Row L-R: Albert Cameron and Richard Weibe, guitars. Alf Walsh, leader and fiddler. Claude Stubley, bass and MC. Vern Braaten, accordion player. Bottom Row L-R: Singing Sweethearts, Diane Rueb and Ardith Bielman. Chuck Gullion, steel. "Sparkles" Stubley and Richie Walsh, vocal. Front: Eddie Stevens, vocal.

The studio also produced music by the rock group called the Dynamics which was lead by Bjarne Larsen.

Back L-R: Larry Stefanyk on Bass, Jeff Mahaffey on guitar, Front L-R: Brian Chamberlain on keyboards, Bill Padley on drums and Guitarist Bjarne Larsen.

Besides TV, you could catch them playing at Di's Pizza on the weekends with the addition of Jim Stenhouse as the lead singer. Their music could be heard at many teen dances surrounded by a large following of teenagers. Great music from very accomplished musicians.

Music Scene in the Peace Country

It is indeed an honor and privilege to compile this history of my involvement in the music scene over the years.

I grew up in Southern Ontario, starting piano lessons at age 8. I studied in the Royal Conservatory of Music classical piano program and had completed grade 9 at age 15 (which is 2 years away from a degree in piano). I had wonderful teachers who pushed and encouraged me. I was fortunate to skip a few grades in the program allowing me to achieve this lofty goal at a young age. I moved to Chilliwack BC in 1958 with my family and performed in my first band (a Country Band) in 1959.

In the summer of 1960 I found myself in Fort St. John at age 18. After a few months of meeting new friends I sat in with a few bands, playing gigs around town for the next one and a half years. I had little or no experience but was absolutely driven to be a performing musician.

My early influences were Jerry Lee Lewis, Ray Charles, Floyd Cramer and Charlie Rich. I spent countless hours studying their chord voicings and practicing until I had their styles down. Along the way I met several keyboard performers who taught me blues chord voicings and licks that helped immensely in developing my style. In the spring of 1961 I entered a talent show in Dawson Creek that was televised on CJDC TV and was fortunate to win. Later that year I was at a dance in Fort St. John where "The Volcano's" from Dawson Creek were playing. I heard someone call my name. It was Bill Padley (drummer for the group) who had seen me competing on the talent show and asked if I would consider joining the "Volcano's". I joined the band shortly thereafter. The members of that band were Bjarne Larsen (rhythm guitar & lead vocals), Jeff Mahaffey (Sax) Paul Jorgensen (Bass Guitar) and Bill Padley (drums). This band folded in 1962.

In the summer of 1963 I joined one of the best bands I have ever performed with, "Barney & the Dynamics". The original members were Bjarne Larsen (lead vocals), Jeff Mahaffey (lead guitar), Jack Wilson (rhythm guitar), Larry Stefanyk (bass guitar), Bill Padley (drums). Unfortunately Bill broke his wrist shortly after the band was formed and was replaced by Arden Hillman. The Dynamics competed in a "Battle of the Bands" in the summer of 1964, performing before a huge crowd in the arena and were honored by winning. The band was very popular in the Peace Country, ironically so heavily booked out of town, rarely performing at home. I left the band in the spring of 1965.

In July of 1966 I entered the "Centennial Search for Talent, (televised on CJDC TV Dawson Creek). I was fortunate to win the regional title, allowing me to compete at the finals in Vancouver. The competition was fierce resulting in winning runner up. The experience was priceless. In 1968 I formed "The Inn Crowd" with original members, Jim Stenhouse (lead vocals) Laine Dahlen (rhythm guitar & vocals) and Bill Padley (drums). Bill eventually moved away and was replaced by Frank Dryden. The "Inn Crowd" was together for several years eventually folding in 1970.

The Inn Crowd
Frank Dryden,   Bryan Chamberlain,   Laine Dahlen,   Jim Stenhouse

In March of 1969 Kelly Piccinin and I purchased the Music Centre in Dawson Creek. Originally operated as Kelly DeYong Sound Centre, later becoming Ye Olde Music Shoppe. I bought Kelly out in 1976, moved the store to a much larger location on 102 avenue and operated until 1983 when the business closed. It was a great pleasure to be in the music business and I received phenomenal support from musicians far and wide.

From 1970 to 1978 I was honored to be a part of "The Knight Express" later becoming "Express". Over the years we had many band members come and go. Jim Stenhouse, Marty Wolsey & Bjarne Larsen (vocals), Ray Jeanotte, Barry Thompson & Mike Saunders (bass guitar), George Hauser, Noel Byrnes, Bill Lalonde, Merv Bauman & Tim Burles (lead guitar). Express was the house band at Di's Steakhouse and the Blue Boar Inn. At one point we did 27 months, three nights a week at Di's and never took a break. If one of the band members was away we simply slotted in a musician that we were comfortable with. I took a hiatus from performing for a few years, joining "Pilot" in 1981. Band members were Caroline Grant (vocals), Gary Gilbertson (lead guitar & vocals) Shannon Anderson (bass guitar & vocals) and Brad Neste (drums & vocals).

I moved away from Dawson Creek in the summer of 1983. In 2006 I was contacted by Ray Jeanotte to see if we could resurrect any or part of "Express" for a Notre Dame High School reunion. It took some doing but we managed to get Jim Stenhouse, Ray Jeanotte, Merv Bauman, Bill Padley and myself together. We rehearsed for a week and ended up performing at "Rockwell's", (the old Di's) on the Thursday night of that week to the same fan base from about 1974. We performed the wind-up dance for the reunion on the Saturday night.

In summary, I believe that I had the honor of performing with some of the best musicians in Canada over the years and it was a privilege to a part of the music scene in Dawson Creek. Sadly Jack Wilson, Bjarne Larson and Bill Padley have passed on. They were great friends and musicians and are dearly missed.

Bryan Chamberlain

Dawson Creek also produced the band known as the Nighthawks. This band was also very popular with the teens and played at many dances in halls throughout the region. These fellows were also very accomplished musicians and singers.

Roger Regnier, Vocals and Guitar, Adley Callison, Lead Guitar, Ray Jeannotte, Bass Guitar and Back-Up Vocals, Harry Redmond, Lead Guitar and Back-Up Vocals, Neil McMahon, Lead Guitar and Back-Up Vocals, Ed Regnier, Drums and Back-Up Vocals, Leo Regnier, Lead Guitar and Back-Up Vocals and Paul Regnier, Bass Guitar and Back-Up Vocals.

There were other bands and musicians that flourished in Dawson Creek like: Tony and the Tone Benders.

Al Bishell, Leonard Neville, Tony VanUden, Ray Jeannotte and Harry Redman.

Another group to emerge was Davie and his Dynamics; It consisted of:

Kerry Dube (Drums), Andy Girard (Vocals), Tony Girard (Vocals), Charlie Larson (Keyboard & Backup Vocals), Pete Nepstad, (Lead Guitar), Alvin Stedel (Bass & Backup Vocals).

Chuck Nahumko was hired as a DJ at CJDC. This job suited his personality, his love for music as well as his ability to talk the talk. He loved to have his friends call him when he was working and request songs to be dedicated to their girl/boy friends. Julie McGowan once won a 45 record for being the first to phone in to Chuck's program with the correct spelling of his name. He was Dawson Creek's answer to "Wolfman Jack." Chuck went on to be a radio personality in Edmonton as "Chuck Chandler."

While working for a Montreal radio station, he broadcast his show from the bedside of John Lennon and Yoko Ono in 1969.

CJDC supported the community in a number of ways that included local interest groups. If you had a pig to sell or a room to rent, you could phone the radio station and go on air to advertise your item. They would announce church services, garage sales or anything that was happening in the local area.

Chuck Nahumko, AKA Chuck Chandler

Across the street from the radio station, was the Peace River Block News. It was originally located in Rolla; a small community located about 10 miles north of Dawson Creek. The building and its printing equipment were moved to the north east corner of 9th st. and 102 ave. of Dawson Creek after the NAR railhead was established in 1932. This business was owned and operated by the Kitchen family. It operated for many years delivering the printed news to the residents of Dawson Creek.

There were many thriving businesses lining 102 avenue; There was the glass shop owned by Mel Olsen, Zwicks Plumbing and Heating, Singer Sewing owned by Willy Evenson, the New Palace Hotel and Café owned by Mah Show and Mah Fang, Wilk's Jewellers owned by Walter Wilk. The Lakeview Credit Union, with long-time manager Gunner Mortensen, was next to the Legion. Bill and Pearl Beadle had a lunch counter between the radio station and the Mile Zero hotel. Edmond Eby was a barber in a little shop in the same vicinity. Paul Nahumko had his tailor business in a small shop between the New Palace Hotel and the Block News. In the next block west of 10th street housed businesses like Kittson's Drugs on the corner; the Five to a Dollar store next to it (later to become Saan store).

Mile Zero Hotel, Canadian Legion, Credit Union

In the downtown core there was a Five Cents to a Dollar Store. It was owned by McKenzie's (Bert, as I recall). They had four children Karen, Gordon, Edith and Bruce. Edith and I were the same age and friends starting school. The store was located on the south side of 102nd Ave. next-door to where the Mile Zero Cafe was... between the back alley and Kittson's Drugstore. Mrs. McKenzie passed away and I heard that Mr. McKenzie passed away about a year later. One of the children went to live with Mittons. I believe the store location changed then to next door to Mittens Florists, the north side of 102nd Avenue and they ran it or a while.

<u>*Donna Field-McLeod*</u>

So, when the Five Cents to a Dollar Store was beside Mittens Florists, I was sent downtown by Mom, with a $20 bill to buy school supplies for myself and 2 brothers. It was independence that I had grown to enjoy. I think I was 12. I had the cards we got in the mail in late August from the school.

In that store, I sat my wallet down and never saw it again. It was a big responsibility buying things, shopping carefully. Money didn't come easily and when it was used up there was no Charge Card, no 'Overdraft', no Line of Credit. I was embarrassed that I was careless when I knew well, how important $20 was. (I got 50 cents an hour for babysitting. We got new clothes for school in the Fall plus coats, boots, shoes only when needed. I used my own money to buy extras like fabric to sew for myself.) I didn't get scolded. Mom somehow found me money to go down again to shop for what was on those supply lists. I asked at the store a few times hoping my wallet had been found. Mom very likely didn't tell my dad.

Julie McGowan-Skead

Next to Dollar store was a small music store which was owned by Harry Noakes and his wife. This little store is where one could purchase the latest records that were being played on the radio. I purchased my first 45 record there; it was "Honeycomb" by Jimmy Rogers. I shared the cost of one dollar and the record with my neighbour and friend Terry Roberts who lived down the block from me. It was a unique buying experience; you could take the record into a booth and play it before purchasing. The store also had sheet music and various instruments for sale.

Webb's Men's Wear was just across the alley from the music store, I believe it was once a general store prior to being a men's wear. Lawrence's Meat Market was in the same block and had been there since the beginning of time. Joe LaFond worked there as a butcher and eventually bought out Lawrence.

Next to Lawrence's Meat was Jack Patterson's Men's Wear.

Jack Patterson's Men's Wear

Doug Patterson sits in the back of what was once his father's store, surrounded by piles of merchandise that will soon be sold at clearance prices. He is explaining why, after supporting three generations of his family, the business must soon close. He repeats that economic stress is not the major factor, Jack Patterson's Menswear simply ran out of family members willing to take over the store. Originally a community general store founded by Jack Patterson, Doug's uncle, the merchandise shifted to menswear in 1945. In 1962, Brennan took control with partner Gus Patterson, Jack's brother and Doug's father. Doug bought his father's share of the business in 1980, and has run the business with Brennan ever since. But now, with Brennan about to retire, Patterson says he simply can't run the store alone.

Excerpt from the files of the South Peace Historical Society

On the north side of the street was the Rec Center. It was owned by Roy and Nello Ravelli, who had built a pool hall in the basement of the building. They had moved their pool hall from it's long-time location next to the Dawson Hotel. I remember playing pool one day in the old location, when my father walked in. I was there at a time when I was supposed to be in school. My dad asked if he could join me in a game; I said, "Sure, grab a stick". After a couple of hours of "bonding", he decided it was time to go home. On his way out he turned and said "I don't think you will ever make a living at playing pool; perhaps you should go back to school and get an education." Very subtle, but that's the way my dad was!

There was a stationery store, a bank, a drugstore and a hardware store in the same block. Floyd Wilson was the first fire chief and owned Wilson's Grocery in the middle of this block. His son Jackie played guitar and played with a couple of the local bands. On the same side of the street, but west of 11th street, was the Windsor Hotel...spent many hours of pub crawling there. Farther along the street was Leach's Tire; I worked part time there after school and on weekends. Don Leach was a very nice man and a pleasure to work for. I worked very hard for my pay, busting truck and tractor tires that were filled with calcium chloride. (which was used in tractor tires as a ballast.) That stuff was very hard on the hands and clothes. On paydays I would quickly find a way to spend my money.

Don and Dennis Leach

One place I liked to go was next door to Wally's Sporting Goods. Wally was a man who knew everything there was to know about guns and he was not shy about telling you so. The store walls were lined with rifles and shotguns as well as all the latest in fishing gear. Wally had everything one could imagine that could be used in outdoor activities. I had my eye on a semi-auto 22 rifle which I purchased soon after my paycheque was cashed. After getting home with my new purchase, my mother told me she thought I had better things to spend my money on. She was probably right; she was a very wise lady.

Dawson Creek had its share of chain stores like; Woolworth's, Kresge's, Safeway and the Hudson's Bay Co. The Bay purchased the building that was once Harper's, it was owned by Wes Harper (Julie McGowan's grandfather) and employed many people over the years.

"The Hudson's Bay....I modeled for the store for two years....with three other girls...the teen sports line. I think my 'flair' was often manifested in the bizarre clothes I sometimes wore! Add then, UBC and Ryerson Poly Tech in Toronto, where I explored and took hold of my aptitude for design".

Dyanne Kortmeyer-Johnson

"Woolworth's....my first job as a teen, Bobby Viksush and me. It must have been '59 or '60 when I worked there. Bobby and I worked at night cleaning the store. Paid a dollar an hour, I remember, as that was a fair wage in those days. The store wasn't that old at the time, couldn't have been open for long."

Mike Blore

The Bay had a men's wear department which employed two of my friends, Mel Carter and Don Chamberlain. They both took great pleasure in wearing their jacket's and ties to work everyday and they looked very dapper while assisting their customers. The teenage boy's look in apparel was greatly influenced by these two.

The Bay – formerly Harper's Department Store

Chapter Eight

EVERYONE'S GONE TO THE MOVIES

The First movie theatre in Dawson Creek was the Northland Theatre. It was originally called the Carlsonia. It was located on the southwest corner of 11th street and 102nd avenue, across from the Windsor hotel. The structure included an upper balcony which was usually occupied by teenage boys and girls who didn't spend a lot of time watching movies. Smoking was allowed in the theatre then and there were times when I was amazed that the projector light could penetrate the smoke filled room to reach the screen.

This was the place where kids would go on a Saturday afternoon to watch the stories unfold on a screen before their very wide eyes. In the early fifties, thirty five cents would get you admission, a bag of popcorn, and a pop. It was pandemonium as kids sat impatiently waiting for the movie to begin. Once the lights went down there was a huge roar of cheers from a packed house, only to be followed by a chorus of loud boos when the World News came on the screen. Nobody came to see the news, bring on the cartoons! Besides the cartoons like "Heckle and Jeckle", "Mighty Mouse" and "Woody Woodpecker", there were always the short subject films; including the likes of the "Three Stooges", "The Bowery Boys", and "Spanky and The Gang". The serial movies like "Superman" with its "to be continued" were sure to bring you back the following week.

The billboards in the lobby displayed the attractions for the upcoming weeks. One had to see the newest adventure of Tarzan or the latest from Gene Autry, Roy Rogers and Hopa-Long Cassidy.

The Northland Theatre, formerly the Carlsonia

The Tarzan series added to the file in my brain, that held scary predicaments from westerns...the unbearable scene of captive Jane tied down while an elephant was about to step with its thousands of pounds, on her face! I was never certain that Tarzan would arrive in time, so when this incident occurred in following episodes, I clamped my eyes shut! (as I do to this day in movies) I think I was 8 or 9. One Saturday my brother and I had walked to the swimming pool to find it closed for cleaning. So, dressed in swimming suits and carrying only our towels, we had convinced ourselves that Mom wouldn't mind if we walked straight over to The Northland and spent our money there. I can still feel the insecurity I kept inside while smiling and acting confident on the outside, standing in line on the sidewalk in my swimming suit with my towel over my shoulders. (Now I think, 'You deserved to feel uncomfortable. It wouldn't have been suggestive, but, small town or not, that wasn't suitable attire.')

Julie McGowan-Skead

Tarzan...a girl's imagination, too! Our swing in the backyard....yes! My dad (early oil exploratory work North of Dawson and into Alberta) made that swing out of drill stem. I cracked and dislocated both my ankles attempting to swing like Tarzan from that very high top pipe! Hmmmm... crippled me for almost a year!

Dyanne Kortmeyer-Johnson

The Vogue theatre was located on the northeast corner of 12th Street and 102nd Avenue. It was built later than the Northland. I think they must have had better connections to the movie distributors as they would show the latest films available at the time. It had much more comfortable seats and could hold more people than its competitor; but somehow it did not have the same ambiance.

I would leave the theatre on a late summer afternoon having just watched a western movie starring John Wayne. I went out the back door, across Alaska avenue, and into the field next to the tracks. I rode my horse across the grass filled prairie, constantly looking around for the bad guys, slapping my horse on the hind quarters. It didn't matter that the hind quarters I were slapping were my own!

The Ten Commandments was released in 1956 and I think it may have been the first film I saw in VistaVision. It had a large cast of stars and ran for three hours and forty minutes, it was so long it had an intermission in the middle of the screening. It was an epic film directed by Cecil B DeMille and it remains one of my all time favourites to this day.

Ben-Hur came out in 1959 and played on the screen of the Vogue theatre, thrilling the audience with the chariot race scene. It was another great movie.

Most kids my age (10 or 11 years old) did not really like musical movies, didn't, I'm not sure about the girls. But there were some great musicals that came out in the fifty's such as the Wizard of Oz. (I know it was released in 1939, but it was re-released in 1955) Everyone knows "Somewhere Over The Rainbow", sung by Judy Garland and reprised by many on TV shows like American Idol and The Voice.

"Oklahoma" was released in 1955 starring Gordon MacRae and contained many great songs by Rogers and Hammerstein, such as: The title song "Oklahoma", "Oh, What A Beautiful Mornin", and "The Surrey With the Fringe On Top". I thoroughly enjoyed watching and listening to Billy Crystal perform this song in "When Harry Met Sally". I found this movie (Oklahoma) and it's music to be so inspiring, that I rushed down to Noakes music store to purchase the sheet music for it. I was taking piano lessons at the time from Mrs Jack Tucker and I wanted to learn to play this great music.

The Vogue Theatre after it was purchased by the Elks

The Crest theatre opening sounded the death knell for the Northland theatre. It was not too different from the Vogue theatre with one unique difference; they started showing movies at midnight on Sunday evenings. At that time the law prohibited movies house from opening on Sunday. The only way around this, was to open on Monday morning at one minute after midnight. I am still amazed at the number of people who participated in this event.

The Ranch Drive-in was opened in 1959. It was located on the Pouce Highway just a little south of town. Watching a movie while sitting in the comfort of your own car, was truly unique; especially for those of us who practically lived in our cars.

One of the complications of showing a movie in Dawson Creek at an outdoor venue, was the fact that the sun did not go down until 11:00 PM in May and June and only marginally earlier in July and August. I guess that really did not matter all that much to most of the male and female patrons in attendance, as their attention was focused elsewhere for most of the movie.

They would show a double feature on every night, the first one was not an Oscar winner, so it really didn't matter that the first half of the movie was washed out by sunlight.

The snack bar was as good as they get, serving hamburgers, french fries and hot dogs, as well as the regular theatre staples like popcorn etc.

The last showing of a movie on the big screen of the Ranch Drive-in Theatre was in October of 1981.

Dollar-a-Carload night....no seat-belt laws, so...lots of bodies...some in trunk but not supposed to be...could get checked. In the summer, 'dark' had a new meaning. The wide prairie sky was often a clear and bright navy blue filled with stars. When I was 16 an early Sunday morning fishing trip was planned following the double feature at the drive-in. I was dropped off at home, still daylight, had an hour and a half to sleep, and was picked up at 5 AM. daylight, by 2 other couples and my boyfriend, to fish the Sukunka! (The dedication was tied to keeping a boyfriend, not to fishing!)

Julie McGowan-Skead

I remember Ardith Bielman being the cashier at the Crest. The pop machine dispenser....pop was in little cups back then. I also remember the girls walking up and down the aisles with their flashlights. The twinkling stars in the ceiling. The FRESH popcorn. I saw Elvis' first movie at the Crest with my Aunt Ethel. Who remembers the "intermission" when a long movie was showing? I also remember double features at the Vogue Theatre.....Who I remember is Mr. Magoo, The Three Stooges, The Lone Ranger. Many years ago when I was in grade one, my mum used to pick my brother and I up from school and go to a Wednesday afternoon movie.....my mum, now 97, remembers the kids are pointing their fingers at the screen....they were right into the western movie being shown.

Susan Wood-Jensen

Chapter Nine

CHEESEBURGER IN PARADISE

Once entering junior high school, it was no longer cool to be bringing your lunch to school in a brown paper bag or a Superman lunch box. The only option was to find a place to buy a hamburger and fries which did not include the school cafeteria. Fortunately their was Ben's White Spot located across the street from both the junior and senior high schools. There was a mad rush to get in the door at lunch time as it was not a very large establishment. Ben Bonnet was the owner and along with his wife they put out a fine hamburger for the cost of thirty five cents. But more important than food was the entertainment that was happening while we ate. The jukebox was belting out songs and the guys and girls were dancing to tunes like: "At The Hop" by Danny and the Juniors, "Peggy Sue" by Buddy Holly, "Little Bitty Pretty One" by Thurston Harris and "Rockin' Robin" by Bobby Day as well as many others. The Jive was the rage at this time and these kids knew how to do it, even Ben had to stop and admire them as they danced, all the time smiling from ear to ear.

No café was ever without a jukebox and his was no different. At noon hour this establishment was filled to capacity with teenagers, all the new dance steps were being demonstrated and the sound levels far exceeded the legal decibel levels. The smoke was so thick it could be cut with a knife. The high school kids had dibs on who got in and who didn't. Ben was a fairly big chap and was well respected by most. He had a big heart as well as frame. If for some reason you were a little short on cash he would bank roll you until you had some. No one, and I mean no one, ever stiffed him.

Keith Skead

When school was let out, we were greeted and treated by Smittie's blue chipmobile parked on the street beside the high school. It was a converted truck which resembled a class c motor home with the original front end and a square structure built on the rear. Inside housed Smittie's deep fryer and his chipping machine along with a large supply of potatoes. This man knew how to make french fries and for twenty five cents you could get a cone piled high with golden brown fries. He also supplied a larger square container filled with those delicious fries for fifty cents. The only other thing on his menu was a pronto pup, which was a wiener on a stick that was coated in a batter then deep fried. It was also a mouth watering delight. The only condiment that he supplied was vinegar as it was the traditional way to eat fries in Great Britain.

In the evenings you could find this blue chipmobile parked on the corner by Kittson's drug store, with him inside reading a book under a Coleman lamp waiting for his next customer.

Smittie started out in a small cafe across the street from the Crest theatre and progressed from there to his chipmobile. His next venture was to purchase McBee's drive-in restaurant which he turned into Mr. Smittie Drive-in.

Smittie's Chipmobile...I would never ask for a chip from a friend...just hope they offered me one. I had a normal-sized packed lunch but was always still hungry those teen years. If I bought chips I didn't really want to give up even one. My allowance or babysitting money seemed better spent on material for sewing clothes. (Also, I often had an item of clothing on lay away at The Bay where I worked part time, paying towards it 50 cents to a dollar at a time.) I remember telling Mom about the Chipmobile all of a sudden being gone and her saying the City likely took away his business licence because of litter.

Julie McGowan-Skead

Smittie Drive-in, Formerly McBee's

My dad rented McBee's Drive-In Restaurant from the owner, Mr. Thompson, (Mom thinks it might have been David) and called it Len's Drive-In. I worked for my mom and dad at the drive-in. They couldn't have made much money, as I was told how much mix and how much milk to use for the milkshakes and I ignored the instructions and made them richer and thicker with more of the 'mix' and less milk! And, I used to give the cooks a hard time. What did they expect? I was only 14 when I started! They also ran the Alaska Cafe. I worked for them there, too.

Gail Walters-Rasmussen

Another drive-in café to come on scene was one called "Mr. Smittie." The establishment came to be as a result of one ambitious man. Smittie started out selling French Fries out of a small van that he had converted to a food truck. He would park the truck between our two schools and sell french fries. For twenty five cents you got a paper cones worth. For fifty cents you received a small box full. He would be on site at noon and after school until the students had gone home for the day. At his drive-in he increased his product line to selling hamburgers, fries, pop, onion rings etc. It is reputed that he made the best hamburgers in the world, well, to us he did. On one occasion my good friend Leonard Ashlee and I were on a flying trip from Prince George to Dawson. As we approached the city, Len asked if Smittie's was still there? I assured him it was, so a stop there appeared to be next on the flight plan. Hitchhiking a ride from the airport to town we headed straight to Smittie's for his renowned hamburger. Sometime later we were met by another of our good friends Murray Logan. Asking us what we would like to do we in unison replied "take us to Smittie's for a hamburger." Only after consuming our food did we fess up and told him this was our second of the day.

Keith Skead

Chris Smith (Smittie) was of Scottish ancestry and besides his culinary skills, he was an accomplished bag piper. For as long as I can remember, Chris Smith and the rest of the Dawson Creek pipe band, led every parade down the streets of Dawson Creek. Smittie contributed much of his time and talent to enrich the lives of the citizens of our community.

After an evening of carousing, many of us would stop at the Alaska Chicken Inn for a coffee and a snack before heading home for the evening. The place was on Alaska Avenue beside a truck stop and was usually full of people enjoying the food and beverages. Dee Stewart was always there in the evenings taking orders from customers; taking cash at the till, directing her staff to people waiting for service. She would also be checking on orders with the kitchen and often lifting her glasses from the string around her neck to read something on a guest check. My favourite dish on her menu was the chili and toast.

Like many other business owners in Dawson Creek, Mrs. Dee Stewart was very hard working and was the sole reason for the success of this business. Unfortunately the Chicken Inn and the truck stop next-door were destroyed by fire in November of 1972.

Chicken Inn next to the Esso

Mann's Cafe was located on 8th street and 104 avenue and was owned by Joe Mann. This was another late evening pit stop for the midnight prowlers. Besides the cafe, Joe also had a motel, service station, and a garage. Joe junior was a friend from school days.

I remember Jean and Curly's restaurant who served great home cooking. Always gifts for all kids at Christmas time. It was located about a block from Central school and across the street to the east. It would have been about mid-fifties. (Later to become Ben's White Spot.)

I remember Ben's White Spot very well. I went there everyday after school all through elementary school to check in with my mother who worked there. (I do have an old staff photo)

The Stewarts ran the truck stop cafe on Alaska Avenue and was renowned for its clam chowder!

In junior high at Central we could hardly wait to go for lunch to buy from the "Chipmobile" owned and operated by Chris Smith who also owned Smittie's Drive-in burger restaurant located on Alaska Avenue.

High school hangouts were the Starlight cafe and Wing's cafe on the south side of 102 Avenue. Mexican hats (a donut with a scoop of ice cream over the hole) and cokes were the orders of the day.

The Pipe Band took part in the fall fair parade every August. The fair always had lots of exhibits and a rodeo, and carnival with rides and many types of games. As the years went by the exhibits were dropped which I believe was a great loss. Anyone growing up in Dawson of course knew about the big July 1 barbeque in Pouce Park. It always started with a parade. The Dawson Creek Pipe Band always took part in local parades. I remember Dave Spittal (of Spittal's Meats) on the big bass drum and Chris Smith (yes, from the chipmobile) on the bagpipes. There were many others in the band but the names are long gone from my memory.

Ben's White Spot (circa 1955)
Mae Schneider, Nellie Doyle, Gwen Moore

Wing's Cafe (Cabaret) was a favourite after-school stop for many high-school students. A plate of french fries with gravy and a bottle of coke was a mouth watering favourite. Someone would put a quarter in the jukebox, and we would sit and listen to the music of Elvis, Buddy Holly and many other popular tunes of the day. Our purchase had its limits on the amount of time Jack Wing would let us sit there. He would boot us out in time to make our way home for supper.

Just west of Wing's was the Starlite Cafe which was owned by Pete Wing and Harry Dar; it was not as popular with teens as Wing's, but did it's share of business. Pete Wing came to Dawson Creek in 1942 and spent the rest of his life here.

The New Palace Hotel and Cafe was one of the longest established businesses in town and was run by Mah Show and Mah Fang. It was one of the best places to go for Chinese food. The building originally was Harper's Store and was purchased from Wes Harper in the early forties. Mr. Harper constructed a new store on the corner of 10th st and 103rd avenue.

The Alaska Hotel Cafe was run for a time by Len Walters and was always full of hungry customers enjoying the fine meals put on by the cooks in the back.

Most of the hotels had their own restaurant or cafe to serve their guests and there was no shortage of coffee shops in town.

Alaska Hotel & Cafe

New Palace Hotel & Cafe

Next door to Empire Cleaners was the Dairy Queen which was opened and operated by the Kortmeyers. It had the best soft ice cream, banana splits, and milkshakes. This business was later purchased by Ray Downie and he continued to run it for a number of years.

Dairy Queen on 102 Ave

Dad built the A&W first. The boys worked with Dad at the A&W. The Dairy Queen was Dad's second project. It was to be Mother's domain. They won international awards for the cleanliness and the production of the highest standard of food in both the Dairy Queen and A&W. I worked alongside my mother, but if things got too busy at the A&W I was switched to being a car hop. Saturday nights after closing, we would pick up an A&W order, take our DQ desserts and go and watch the SILENT drive-in pictures from the side of the road!

A & W on Alaska Avenue

I remember fondly the "TAIL" ends of a few movies! My Dad then built a Dairy Queen in Prince George, which my Uncle and Aunt supervised and, built Corlane Sporting Goods in Dawson, and hired a manager to run things there. Mom and Dad worked approximately 17 hrs a day for 17 years without a holiday. He was 55 when he retired, Mom 49. They developed a love for exploring rivers… became river rats, and Dad's interest in something else materialized. During his drilling years he'd noticed many unique archaeological phenomena. When the Hudson's Hope dam was being developed he approached the BC government about rescuing dinosaur prints before they were flooded, but found the Tyrell Museum more interested. So for a number of years out of Hudson's Hope he ferried and helped Phil Curey find and retrieve a rare site, giant Ammonite fossils so big they had to be conveyed by helicopter out to Alberta. One very notable find by Dad, was bird prints; he kindly stepped back and let a young archaeologist take the credit. I enjoyed working one summer on the dig with university students, dynamic explorers. Dad taught them how to cut the prints out, had contributed to naming 4 dinosaurs, even was referred to in correspondence as Dr. Kortmeyer...perhaps his 'footprint', kind of a silent one.

Dyanne Kortmeyer-Johnson

Bygone Beaneries

A topic which has been stewing in my mind for quite some time has been the gradual disappearance of various landmark eating establishments in our area over the years. I have been mentally masticating upon the many new restaurants that have recently opened their doors in Dawson Creek to add variety of fare and warmth of surroundings to the ever-changing cafe scene.

Travel back in time with me if you will, and remember a few of the eateries that have vanished from the local landscape.

In some instances the proprietorship and name changed while the restaurant remained in the same location, or later was rebuilt after being destroyed by fire.

Following the Dawson Creek fire and explosion of February 1943, the Five-Cent to a Dollar Store on the corner of 102nd Avenue and 11th Street (now where the Sunlite Cafe is located), was remodeled and became the American Lunch. In July 1945, Walter and Henry Wright bought the cafe, changed the name to the Arcadian Cafe and operated the business until 1947. They sold out and the restaurant became the Pacific Cafe, and later the Starlite Cafe operated by Pete Wing and Harry Dar.

For many years the Wing's Cabaret was located where the Pagoda Restaurant now stands and was owned and operated by Jack Wing and Bill Der.

The Milk Bar was originally operated by the Fletchers and Carberrys, then Kay and Bill Miller took over and later moved the business west on 102nd Avenue in the Peter's Home & Auto Building.

The Royal Cafe was located where the Saan Store is today, and was later purchased by Paul Mah and was moved to 17th Street where it became the Mile One Cafe.

Going farther east along 102nd Avenue (on the site of the Mile Zero Hotel) the old Maple Leaf Hotel was remodeled and became the Shangri-la & Spanish Grill which operated from 1943 to 1945 when it was purchased by Aurele Carriere and became the Bluebird Cafe.

The Bluebird Cafe was later moved to Alaska Avenue where the Travelodge now stands, and still later was moved to Pouce Coupe and converted into a rooming house which was destroyed by fire in January 1980.

On the north side of 102nd Avenue where VanHoy Stationers is today, was Chick's White Lunch.

In 1943 Mah Show and Mah Fong purchased the old Harper's Store on the corner of 102nd Avenue and 10th Street (where the Bank of Montreal now stands), and opened and operated the New Palace Hotel and Cafe until 1967.

Going farther west along 102nd Avenue in the Dudley & Wilson Building was Smittie's

Pancake House, which later became the Colonial Restaurant. Young's Coffee Shop was located farther west on 102nd Avenue where the Windsor Hotel now stands.

The Empress Cafe was located on 10th Street where the Park Hotel stands today. Ben's White Spot was situated in the same building as the Alaska Cafe is today, and was operated by Ben Bonnet at that site in 1951-52, before moving south to where the School Board Offices now stand. Ben then operated under the same name in premises formerly occupied by Jean & Curly's which was run by Jean and Curly Freeman in 1950-51.

On the present Royal Bank corner was Bert's Fish & Chips operated by Bert Graham for many years.

The Alaska Chicken Inn was located on Alaska Avenue west of the Travelodge and was owned and operated by Dee and Bill Stewart until it was destroyed by fire in November 1972. In the west tend of town was Pinky's and Smitties's Burger Bar. Mann's Cafe was located at 10412-8th Street in what is now Jake's Apartments. On 8th Street in more recent times we have had Dog 'N' Suds drive-in, which later became the Blue Boar Inn and is now the Kingsland Garden Restaurant.

Now, in the more recent past we have witnessed the disappearance of Tastee Freeze, the Hungry Cowboy, and Spaghetti Shack, just to name a few. Nor shall we forget Pouce Coupe where Der Song operated Song's Cafe from 1941 to 1975. Also in Pouce was Brown's Cafe, which delighted he palate from 1954 to 1970, under the proprietorship of Gertie and Jim Brown For many years the Hart Hotel Dining Room at Pouce Coupe was the home away from home for many a hungry traveler.

These and many other coffee shops, snack counters, hotel restaurants, and various eateries have passed into time, and only remain as fleeting memories.

Day Roberts (1968

Excerpt from the files of the South Peace Historical Society

Chapter Ten

BURNING DOWN THE HOUSE

The loud wail of the siren from on top of the fire hall on 103rd avenue was the signal to all the volunteer firefighters to get up from the comfort of their beds, and rush to the fire hall. Something was burning! It was the most terrifying sound that one could hear in the middle of the night. The up and down pitch of the sound was disturbing to those of us who were awakened from a sound sleep. For the residents who had survived the bombing of London and were now living here, it must have been like reliving a horror not long past.

The early morning of Christmas Eve in the winter of 1956 was just such an occasion. My father was usually the first person up and over to the window of my bedroom to try and locate the source of the disturbance. We lived on Grandview Heights and had a perfect view of the city. This fire was easy to spot; the entire roof of the Memorial Arena was ablaze. I watched as large pieces of the metal roof flew upward from the heat generated by the inferno. The fire trucks and volunteers raced to the scene but their chances of putting this one out were very slim; the building was totally engulfed by the time they got there. We watched in silence as the fire slowly burned itself out.

In the daylight one could see that all that remained were the concrete block walls of the perimeter, the inside was totally gutted.

The most talked about tragedy (at least by those who were old enough to remember) to take place in Dawson Creek, was the explosion and fire of 1943. A complete city block was destroyed by the burning and subsequent explosion of a building that housed cases of dynamite.

Aftermath of the Explosion in 1943

On February 13, 1943, the only buildings in town that remained without gaping windows, fallen chimneys, crazily twisted doors or smashed-in walls were those isolated buildings of the original village. The hundreds of shacks, bunkhouses, warehouses, and administration buildings which had sprung up in those fields also survived. Northwest of the main intersection, by ten o'clock on that terrible evening, only one wrecked and looted building remained, the old Dawson Co-op Union store. All the rest lay under a smouldering mass of debris where sporadic bursts of flame consumed what little was left of the main business section.

Excerpt from the files of the South Peace Historical Society

The explosion was from a construction company's storing of dynamite, (not the army's) for use in ongoing work on the Alaska Highway.

I was in Edmonton at Alberta College with my friend, Merna Collins. Her two older sisters had a Beauty Parlour above our store. (Harper's Store, which would one day be The New Palace) We lived above the store. There were also some rooms rented out, and there was a chiropractor. My brother was off in the air force. My younger sister was home. Some people had decided to start hauling out stock in case the fire spread to the store but my dad said no and ordered the doors locked. Some windows upstairs broke but the store didn't catch fire.

Dorothy Harper-McGowan

The Co-op store only survived until 1948 when once again fire struck and razed the building to the ground. It was rebuilt in the same location and again became one of the main supplier of goods to the community of Dawson Creek.

Dawson Co-op Burning in 1948

In February 1957, Highway Motors was destroyed by fire. MacDonald's Consolidated Warehouse was consumed by a huge fire that levelled a major wholesale supplier of staple goods to the community. I think this fire happened in the late fifties or early sixties. I remember as a child going through the ruins salvaging anything of value that was not destroyed by the fire.

MacDonalds Consolidated Warehouse Burning

Dawson Creek had difficulty keeping it's schools from falling victim to fire; the South Peace Senior Secondary (as it was now called) burned to the ground on January 28th 1966 and the Notre Dame School was lost to fire on Easter Sunday of 1968. The Dawson Creek Elementary was a victim of an alleged arson in 1973. I don't know how many homes and commercial buildings were consumed by fire in the fifties and sixties, but I am sure there were many. Natural gas had been piped in to many homes, but there were still a lot of people heating their houses with wood or coal fires. Wood burning fires created creosote buildup in chimneys and was the cause of many chimney fires. I still remember staying with my cousin Terry Fortin in the back of the old fire hall where he and my uncle Tony lived after my aunt died. My uncle Tony had been a volunteer firefighter for as long as I can remember. Every time I stayed overnight with them I prayed that the terrifying siren would not go off.

South Peace Senior High School Burning in 1966

At 3:30 p.m. on January 28th 1966, over four hundred students of the South Peace Senior Secondary High School trooped out of one of the most modern halls of learning in the north. Over, for the weekend, was the toil of study and classes. Ninety minutes later the high wail of the fire siren caught the ears of many Dawson Creek citizens in the downtown area. The R.C.M.P. shift was changing when the siren went and a constable got the location of the fire over the fire hall intercom as a dispatcher instinctively noted the time at 5:04 p.m., an hour and a half after school had let out. The fire, starting apparently at the southern end of the two-story structure, had almost swept the whole length of the building by the time the first fire department truck arrived. Ninety minutes later, the multi-million dollar plant was declared a total loss.

Excerpt from the files of the South Peace Historical Society

I was a volunteer with the Fire Dept at the time of the high school fire but was a full time FF for the others. Also I believe that the photo of the old hall, which I believe was on 103 Ave in the 1000 block, hangs in the fire hall. A number of years ago we (fire hall) had the Northern Lights College under the direction of Doug Becotte, Carpenter program, build a replica of this building which now is at the Pioneer Village next to man made lake (Rotary Lake). Capt. John Wright (now deceased) and Lt. Allan LaForge were instrumental in this project getting done. Our old 1951 International pumper which was used at the time to fight a number of fires including the elevator fire at Pouce, sits in this building at the village.

Tom Gannon

My dad worked at CNT (Canadian National Telecommunications) in 1966. He called me at home from work and said "The High School is on fire! I will come and pick you up so we can see it!" He quickly drove home at 5:15 that day, picked me up and drove to the fire. We turned at the old Safeway corner of 102nd and 13th then turned at 104th to watch the North doors of the hallway by the gym blow out and flames stretched almost across 104th. After watching the fire for a couple hours we headed home. When we got home our house was full of smoke! I had put potatoes in a pot of water on the stove to boil for supper and forgot to turn the old gas burner off. Luckily we got home in time as the pot was dry and the potatoes were black and smoldering! Never forget that night. I was 13 at the time of the fire. My mother was scheduled to go in to a woodworking night class at the High School that night. She was so upset that her project (can't remember what it was) was lost in the fire.

Blaine Nicholson

1950's Firehall on 103rd Avenue

Dawson Creek Fire Department 1958

Back - Bob Card, Elwood Ashton, Ken Webb, Ray Newby, Bill Schild, Tony Fortin, Bob Blackstock & Bob Trail
Center - Ben Hoy, Don McGowan, George Thorson, Ken MacLem, Chuck Torey, Stan Hill, Bob Johnston, Joe Bodner &
Norm Mytron
Front - Earl Johnson, Bill Foster, Frank Pallson & Art Callihan.

Chapter Eleven

LET IT SNOW

When snow begins to fall, it's not always a welcome sight to everyone, but to most it is the beginning of a new season which brings entertainment and joyful times. Tobogganing, skiing and skating on frozen ponds, like McQueen's slough, was the embodiment of winter fun. Hockey sticks, skates, and pucks were brought out of storage and shinny games flourished on many of the local outdoor rinks. I built a bobsled that had steel runners, and a steering wheel that I purchased from Fred Vosslers auto-wrecking, and mounted it so I could steer to some degree. We would haul this heavy hulk to the top of 100th avenue to jump on and ride it to the bottom. I didn't have the patience to figure out a braking system; so we would send spotters to the bottom of the hill on 8th st to watch for traffic and signal us when it was all clear. There was the odd occasion when this safety method did not work as well as it should have. I came down that hill at a very high rate of speed and crossed 8th st under the belly of an 18 wheeler truck's trailer, scooting out the other side into the NAR field. I was totally unscathed but somewhat shaken by the close brush with death. We abandoned this location and spent much happier times towing it behind a car on deserted country roads.

Snow piled high down the centre of 102nd avenue

The deeper the snow got, the more people resented the task of digging their cars out of a snow bank before being able to go off to work or school. There was also the chore of plugging your car's block heater in before bedding down for the night. If this job was neglected in -30 temperatures, there was a good chance you wouldn't have to shovel out your vehicle in the morning. It wouldn't start!

The city had snowplows that began piling the snow up in the middle of the streets; eventually the snow got so deep that only the tallest of people could see the other side. Somehow this did not deter people from crossing in the middle of the block to get to the other side. I guess climbing over the huge pile of snow was their way of defying winter and not letting this minor inconvenience change their routine. When the snow in the middle piled up so high that it jeopardized the safe flow of traffic, the city brought out the snow blowers and dump trucks to remove it.

Snow piling up on 102nd avenue

And then removing it

When we lived in the West End we would walk over to the Soap Box Derby Hill (Kin Park) with a wooden toboggan that could hold three. There were always kids taking a run and leaping onto pieces of cardboard, a smoother faster ride and much lighter to carry back up to the top! I remember there being an old car hood or a big fender there but wouldn't dare try it out. (my safety conscious dad's nature and mine) We depended on the heat registers to dry out our boots and woolen mitts. (In later years, once plastic bags were 'invented', we could go to school in 'still damp' boots by first putting each foot into a plastic bag!) After we'd moved up to the hill, most of the neighbourhood used the top end of 16th St. that ran by our house, for the start of a long 'run' down to a field that ended in front of Dyke's Construction and Dawson Creek Sash and Door. (96th wasn't very busy...would look both ways, ready to jump off if necessary, as we approached crossing it.) The boys would pack snow up to make 'jumps', which I only experienced when I didn't steer well enough to avoid them!

Julie McGowan-Skead

One of my winter memories is that of sliding down the hill at the south end of the NAR dam (where city hall now is) on a piece of cardboard after school. I believe that dam was created to supply water for the old steam engine locomotives. There was quite a large ditch that ran alongside the dam and in the spring it would be a raging torrent of water. There were some old wooden beams about a foot wide that ran across the ditch and we used to walk across them. If one of us had fallen in it could have been tragic I'm sure.

Errol Erickson

I remember the winter evenings riding sleighs or toboggans on the hill at the back of the house (only when it was warm) no -30 for us. I always thought how lucky that we lived on the hill as we didn't have to go far to sleigh ride!

Judy Moore-Logan

As winter progressed it brought about the season to be jolly. The city had a large collection of Christmas street decorations and soon after the installation on most of the street lamps and the Mile Zero Post, the city took on the most joyous of festive decor. The city put up a very large Christmas tree, usually in the intersection of 102nd avenue and 11th street, and decorated it with hundreds of lights. There was always a Grinch who would try to cut it down in the middle of the night. (Sometimes succeeding.) The City eventually moved it to the center of the traffic circle.

The store windows were all decorated in the various themes of Christmas. If you were lucky enough to drive down 102nd avenue in the very late evening after a heavy snowfall, when the snow was yet to be disturbed by traffic, you would be treated to one of the most beautiful scenes you would ever see in your lifetime.

Christmas was the season when the stores would be filled with shoppers of all ages looking for the perfect gift. Christmas carols would be playing in every store and you could see the excitement building on the faces of everyone.

Mile Zero Post with Christmas Decor

The holiday season was a time for celebration of friends and family. Our house was filled with many friends stopping in to have a glass of cheer and to share in song and laughter. The best and worst time was waiting for my brothers and sister to show up from their homes in other parts of the country. The worst was the waiting, the best was when they finally got there; it was like a scene from "The Walton's Homecoming; a Christmas Story".

We were probably not aware of it at the time but, a lot of the secular Christmas music was recently written and being recorded for the first time in the 50's and 60's. "Blue Christmas" was originally recorded by Ernest Tubb in 1949 and rerecorded by Elvis Presley in 1957. (I liked Porky Pig's version of this as well!)

"Rudolph the Red Nosed Reindeer" was written by Gene Autry and recorded in 1949 and again with an updated version in 1957. "Sleigh Ride" was recorded by it's composer Leroy Anderson in 1950. The instrumental version of this is one of my favourites.

Dennis Day recorded "Christmas in Killarney" in 1950 and it was also successfully recorded by Bing Crosby, Bobby Vinton and Anne Murray. "Silver Bells" was recorded by Bing Crosby in 1950 and covered by too many to list. "It's Beginning to Look a Lot Like Christmas" was recorded by Perry Como in 1952 and Michael Buble's version charted #2 on Billboard's adult contemporary chart in December of 2011.

"Santa Baby" was recorded by Eartha Kitt in 1953 and rerecorded by Madonna in 1987. "Home for the Holidays" was recorded by Perry Como in 1954 and covered by Garth Brooks and Cyndi Lauper in more recent years. "Jingle Bell Rock" was recorded by Bobby Helms in 1957 and is still played to this day every Christmas.

"Rockin' Around the Christmas Tree" by Brenda Lee in 1958 is still one of my all time favourites. "The Twelve Days of Christmas" was originally released by Bing Crosby in 1949 and a more popular version by Mitch Miller in 1961. "It's the Most Wonderful Time of the Year" was released in 1963 by Andy Williams.

"Pretty Paper" was Roy Orbison's contribution to Christmas music in 1963; it was written by Willie Nelson. "A Holly Jolly Christmas" was recorded by Burl Ives in 1964. "Feliz Navidad" by Jose Feliciano and "Merry Christmas Darling" by the Carpenters were both released in 1970 and are regular favourites at Christmas. There have been many Christmas tunes written but few have had the staying power of those from the 50's and 60's.

Christmas Tree at the Mile Zero Post

BC Hydro

Chapter Twelve

TAKE ME TO CHURCH

The church and parishioners of all faiths flourished in Dawson Creek. My commitment to the Anglican Church was enforced by my mother's insistence of my "confirmation" to the Anglican faith. She was very devoted to her belief in Christ and attended church every Sunday. Not so much me. There was just about every denomination of Christianity represented in the City and churches could be found on many streets.

The History of First United Church, Dawson Creek, BC

On a site that had once been the James Paul home at the corner of 104th Avenue and 13th street, the new United Church was built. Mr. Farstad was the architect and Dyke Construction, contractors. The beams each weighed 1350 pounds and it took six men to raise them by block and tackle. Mr. Moffatt, Clerk of Session, and Rev. Reikie got on the cables for the last pull, with Mrs. Reikie looking on. Walter Wright was on hand with his camera. The two story building, 45" x 60"...Dedication Nov. 6, 1955, and Rev. Reikie had received a call to a church in Calgary. Rev. Frank Chubb, the new minister, with his wife, Shirley, arrived in summer of 1956, Dedication of the Sanctuary in Nov. 1956, built by Alsop and Fortin Contractors. The Secretary was Mrs. Millie Best. The Carillons rang out for the first time, and the beautiful new organ pealed forth. The town was growing and with it the congregation. About 30 families were transferred in by Mobile and Imperial Oil Companies around 1956 — 1957. Many of these were United Church members. They were young, well educated, willing to work and were a great acquisition to the church.

Excerpt from the files of the South Peace Historical Society

My dad Bert Moffatt, was often the Santa at the United Church Christmas concerts. But I knew it was my dad. (I would have been pretty young at that time; not sure when I actually figured it out.) My mother was always very involved with the ladies groups putting on Christmas and Mother's Day teas at the church. The Christmas tea always meant mincemeat tarts. So good. Mom headed the afternoon ladies' group -- they called themselves "The West End Busy Bees." Ladies took turns hosting; the lunches at the end of the meeting were something to behold -- sandwiches, cakes, cookies. Aside from talking about Church matters, they also made quilts to go in an emergency pool to help families affected by fires or other misfortune. (Often our living room had a quilting frame stretched out in it.)

Irene DeBoni (nee Moffatt)

OK, Irene, so you kept that part about Santa under wraps! I remember when some friends in Grade 2 said there wasn't really a Santa Claus. I informed them that there WAS, because at the United Church we have a Christmas Concert and Santa comes and gives out bags of candy, and, the Church doesn't lie. I'm glad you didn't tell me it was your dad! The only other time I saw Santa was at a family dance at the Kilkerran Hall....same wee brown paper bags of candy after singing him in loudly with 'Jingle Bells'.

There was a Sunday School picnic every year at Pouce Park 6 miles away, with races and free ice cream cones. My brother and I really looked forward to these, but one time he got left behind. Dad, Mom, I and I believe my baby brother, went in our car to Pouce to get him. He wasn't concerned.....had been exploring, but....there was the river! In Sunday School, during the Collection, we sang, 'Dropping, dropping, dropping, dropping, hear the pennies fall. Every one for Jesus, He shall have them all.' Focussed? I sure was. One penny could buy 3 candies at Pinky's in the West End! Many of us went to church organized camp (Boys' camp a separate location) a few summers at Lake Saskatoon towards Edmonton. I loved it. There was a church choir I was in, with lovely full white cotton attire with Peter Pan collars with black ribbons.

Julie McGowan - Skead

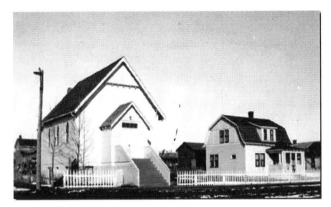

United Church 1945

United Church in the 60's

The Lutheran church which stands on the pointed corner where 103rd and 102nd avenues come together, has been there since about 1938. Carol Ashlee's father and mother, Tarald and Geneva Sandnes, were the first couple to be married in this church on November 29th 1938. I believe that the majority of parishioners that belonged to this church were of Scandinavian decent; but most likely other nationalities as well.

Beside it's service to the Lord, this church served many other functions, the least of which was an annex to the Elementary school across the street. It has survived closure and revitalization over the years and the building still stands today.

Lutheran Church

Another of the long standing churches was the Roman Catholic church which was located on the north west corner of 10th st and 104th avenue. This church and its bell tower can be seen in just about every picture taken of Dawson Creek from the early forties on. My neighbours, who were from the French speaking communities of northern Alberta, were devote Catholics and attended this church on a regular basis. Apparently this church fell victim to fire a some point and I have not been able to confirm the extent of the damage.

Catholic Church

Catholic Church

St Mark's Anglican church is located on the southeast corner of 11th street and 103rd avenue. This church has been in this location for as long as I can remember and was the house of worship for my mother and most of my family over time. My younger brother and I went to Sunday school here and I was later "Confirmed" to the Anglican faith. The Sunday Mass here was not all that different from the Catholic service; I guess Henry VIII did not want to depart too far from the ceremony of Rome.

My father was always a bit suspicious of preachers; and as a result my mother had a difficult time getting him to attend services. He limited his appearances to weddings, funerals and Christmas Eve. He did however find a Reverend "Smith" that he did like and would share a hot rum toddy with him whenever he would come to our house for a visit. I think the thing they had in common was the hot rum drink.

St Mark's Anglican Church

Chapter Thirteen

BLOWING IN THE WIND

Winter months could be long and harsh with temperatures often in the minus 10 to minus 40 degree range. (remembering that this is in Fahrenheit and that 32 degrees above zero was freezing) The magic number was zero and anything above was cold and anything below zero was damn cold. We did receive some relief in the form of that magical phenomenon know as a Chinook.

The wind from the west would form in the Pacific and gather with it the warm air that would travel in the jet stream over the Rocky Mountains and would dive into the regions east of the mountains. The temperature difference could change from -10 degrees to +50 degrees F in as little as a few hours.

This wind could also be a curse as well as a blessing for it often was so strong that it would drift snow over roads and highways fouling traffic for days. There was also the melting of snow that caused slush and pooling of water in the streets and on sidewalks, making walking and driving very difficult. Once the thawing was over, the snow and water would refreeze making travel totally unbearable. This wind would occur intermittently over the winter months, more-so in the latter stages of winter. Anyone who lived in Dawson Creek will remember the winds that persisted in all seasons, we just learned to live with it.

Spring Thaw on 102nd Avenue

I recall when taking flying lessons from Vic Turner in the summer of 1967, I had taken my solo flight and was practicing my crosswind landings into winds gusting to 30 miles an hour. I would do circuits into the wind coming from the south west blowing across the runway, crabbing into the wind with my left wing low fighting to maintain control. I would do a touch and go and come around for another landing. After about 30 minutes of this, I was starting to enjoy the mastery of this challenge. Then on one landing I saw Vic standing by the edge of the runway waving his arms frantically. On the next landing I did a full stop and pulled off the runway to be greeted by Vic; he told me that I should probably stop for the day as the wind was now gusting to over 50 mph.

I never regretted learning to fly in the winds of Dawson Creek, it served me well over the years as flying in wind was never that much of a challenge.

A sure sign that spring was in the air was when the very hardy crocuses began pushing up through patches of snow. Soon the snow was rapidly melting and with it brought on a new batch of problems. The creek began to rise and soon was overflowing its banks and flooding many areas that bordered it. The Kin Park soapbox derby area became a huge lake, almost filling the entire basin. The golf course was totally under water and the culvert under 8th street became plugged with debris and backed up water for many city blocks. The water in the normally docile creek became a raging torrent.

Crocuses pushing up through the snow

The streets and lanes that were not paved, became a mass of very sticky Peace River gumbo. One could walk in gumboots for only a short distance before having to stop and clean off the accumulation of mud before proceeding any farther. I have heard many stories of people who lost their footwear in the deep mud, never to see them again.

Driving was not much better! The spray of muddy water from oncoming cars or worse, trucks, would blind your vision for a seemingly long period of time before windshield wipers would clear a small streaky patch big enough to see through. The service stations had many buckets of water with squeegees sticking out of them; the water in these buckets was almost as dirty as the water running on the streets. It was impossible to drive at night for the headlamps that were covered in mud did not do much to illuminate the road ahead.

Eighth street mud

The winds did provide a somewhat rapid melting of snow and soon the streets were dry. When the streets and yards were sufficiently dried, the wind created a new problem; dust! Dust was everywhere, covering just about everything in town, from cars and trucks to laundry hanging on lines. I had a job at Capital Motors after school and I would wash all of the cars in the lot only to come back the next day to start all over again. It was impossible to find any place or anything in town that was not covered in dust. The streets were covered in dirt from vehicles driving in from rural routes and depositing a trail of mud from their tires. The city street sweepers had the tedious job of trying to clean up this mess; thankfully in time, the streets slowly turned back to normal. Normal did not mean freedom from dust but it became a little more tolerable.

The May long weekend signalled the beginning of planting season. My father always planted a vegetable garden. He would order a load of manure from a local farmer and have Bert Moffatt bring his tractor over to till his garden patch. Bert could not get there soon enough to relieve us from the smell wafting from the garden. My dad spent many hours in his garden; weeding and hoeing the many rows of plants and potatoes. His efforts payed off handsomely in the fall when we reaped the rewards of his green thumb. We ate some of the best vegetables I have ever eaten in my life. Nothing has come close since!

Farmers all around us were soon working their fields and planting crops of wheat, barley, flax and other grains. As spring turned to summer, the grain in the fields and the leaves on the trees turned Dawson Creek and the surrounding area into a beautiful lush green heaven on earth.

Wheat field north of town

For years after moving to the Vancouver area, I always owned or had access to an airplane, and would fly back to Dawson every summer. Passing over the last range of mountains, the sky around me and the ground below me became so clean and clear. It was the most beautiful sight! The summer months produced some of the most intense thunder storms; the likes of which I have not seen anywhere else. Black towering cumulus clouds would form in the west and soon the display of thunder and lightning would be upon us. I loved to go outside and be a part of Mother Nature's best show on earth. Huge lightning bolts came out of every cloud followed by the loudest clap of thunder that would shake the ground below your feet. This was soon followed by a torrential downpour of rain and sometimes hail. The water would start to flow down the streets in streams of violent mass and speed. Thankfully it was over in a relatively short period of time and the damage was minimal.

Tragedy struck one day, to an elderly neighbour, as the result of a thunder storm; lightning struck a power pole in his back yard and the power line to his house came down. In an attempt to move the sparking line away from his home, he grabbed it, only to be electrocuted and cause his immediate death. I gained a new respect for the power of lightning and no longer went into the yard to watch. To this day I still like to watch a good thunder storm.

That pesky, cold wind out of the north reminded us that summer would soon be over. The fields of wheat had turned to a golden brown and the wind brought them to life as it danced over them. The farmers were busy with their equipment ready to cut into the fruits of their labour. The combines began the arduous task of gathering in the sheaves. Soon there was nothing left but the stubble that was once huge fields of grain. The leaves on the trees were now in their fall colors of red, orange and brown clinging to the branches in a last ditch effort to stay a part of summer. This was short lived as the wind once again came in with a mighty blow and stripped everything from the branches. The nights became colder and ice was starting to form on puddles overnight; it was time to get ready to go back to school. The crisp air signalled to us that it was time to go hunting for a moose. It was also a signal to the moose to start looking for a mate and to do its best to avoid us. I think most or at least a lot of people living in Dawson Creek in the 50's and 60's, grew up chewing on a moose or deer steak or a roast that produced the finest drippings for gravy. The meat from these animals was very lean and tasty, it was the epitome of organic food.

First snow fall

Chapter Fourteen

FUNNY HOW TIME SLIPS AWAY

On a trip to Dawson Creek in July of 2015, Carol and I, mostly me, spent many hours at the South Peace Historical Society Archives looking at old pictures of the city. After viewing many of the photos of Dawson Creek past, I decided to take my camera and go on a walkabout. While walking the streets reminiscing and taking pictures, I became aware of how much the city has changed from the "good old days" of the 50's and 60's. There were many landmarks that were no longer there; just vacant lots where many businesses had been. The absence of these buildings brought on a bout of sadness and longing for days gone by.

Calvin Kruk Center (originally the Post Office) the South Peace Historical Society is located in the basement.

When I looked at the building that was once the site of the original Royal Canadian Legion, I remembered that there were many people who were members of this service club who gave of their time and effort supporting local charities and sports. The formation of this club was by and for the service men and women who were veterans of both world wars, and basically anyone who wore the uniforms of those who were there to serve and protect.

The Legion was a place for people to gather to share in a drink, song and laughter. I was too young to be allowed in, but on occasion on cold winter days, I was permitted to wait in the reading room for a ride home. My parents were members and my dad spent many hours behind a mic singing songs from the war years to the delight of many patrons.

He was often accompanied by a couple of French Canadian sisters who sang with him in perfect harmony. (Louise was the wife of Alex Hamel and I don't recall the name of her sister.) My Dad had a beautiful tenor voice and was in demand to perform on many occasions. Quite often the parties migrated to our house after closing time on a Saturday night and the song and laughter would continue into the wee hours. I clearly remember listening to the singing with great admiration.

First Canadian Legion

There was a military presence that lingered well after the 2nd world war in Dawson Creek. The Loran Station was an example of this; it was part of the Distant Early Warning line that was created as a result of the Cold War that existed largely between the US and Russia. The Korean War was a conflict that was raging in the early fifties and had a lot of people fearing an escalation into a 3rd World War. The residents of Dawson Creek seemed to be another world away from this crisis. I remember one morning lying in bed, about to get up to go to school, when I heard a newscast over CJDC, that an American F86 Sabre fighter jet had gone down somewhere in northern B.C. on its way to Alaska. It sent chills down my spine thinking that this war was getting too close to my home.

The Legion must have had great success with it's membership as well as fund raising, as it soon constructed a new and much larger establishment on the south east corner of 9th street and 102nd avenue. When I would come home in the late 60's, I was old enough to get into the lounge, and I could now enjoy playing in crib tournaments with my mother and father.

The financial burden of this building proved to be much more than its membership could endure; the next time I visited, the Legion had moved into a smaller location in the Co-Op mall. This did not last that many years and as a result of waning membership, once more the Legion was on the move. It now found a new location in the curling rink and took over the running of the bar.

The Legion's second home at 9ᵗʰ st and 102ⁿᵈ avenue

At the local bowling alley lounge in July of 2015, Day Roberts explained to me that the Legion could no longer meet the requirements to hold a liquor licence. After more than three quarters of a century, the Royal Canadian Legion Branch 141 was clinging to life with as few as twenty five members.

The NAR station which proudly served our community for years, is now a museum and the only remnant and sole survivor of the once stately grain elevators is now an art gallery.

NAR Station museum

While touring the station museum, I came upon a jukebox remote selector, the kind that was mounted in the booths; the sign above it stated that it came from Wing's Cafe. I suddenly became acutely aware of the passage of time and that I was a part of history for I would have played music from this device in my teen years. A trip upstairs to the bedrooms and a peek into the living room area of the residence area reminded me of parties we had there when Jim Elliott's parents were away at the lake.

Jukebox in the NAR museum

Just south of the station on 10th st and Alaska avenue was a grass covered vacant lot. It was once the location of the Dawson Hotel which became a victim of the wrecking ball in the recent past. Another Hotel which fell by the wayside, was the Windsor; it stood on the corner of 11th street and 102nd avenue from what seemed to be the beginning of time. It was the meeting place for many people after a days work or playing in an evening ball game. I spent many joyful hours there playing pool and drinking the odd pint of beer with many of my friends. It too is now a grass covered vacant lot.

Dawson Hotel

Dawson Hotel vacant lot

Windsor Hotel   **Windsor Hotel vacant lot**

The Windsor Hotel was a Dawson Creek landmark for 54 years. Built in 1951 at a cost of $250,000.00 the hotel had 54 rooms, a modern dining room, 2 beer parlors (one for "Men Only" and the other for "Ladies and Escorts"), a 250 seat banquet room, and room rental rates that were $2.50 a single, to $6.00 a double occupancy per night. Sadly, this grand Dawson Creek landmark endured years of hard times, delinquent property taxes and disrepair. The hotel was taken over by the City of Dawson Creek and unable to find a buyer, it was demolished in 2005. The whole town watched the demolitions and remembered the hotel's better days.

The New Palace Hotel and Cafe, that once stood on the corner of 102nd avenue and 10th street, was no longer to be found. In its place was a new Bank of Montreal. Across the street is Bing's Furniture; it is the building that housed the Co-Op before its move to the new mall east of 8th street. This is a business that was of historical importance and it too was struggling to keep it's head above turbulent financial waters. It was nice to see places like Bill's News & Confectionery still standing in the approximate place it had always been. Farther along 102nd is the building which once housed the Vogue theatre and subsequently the Elks hall, it is now a fitness center. Another vacant lot on the corner of 11th st and 102nd ave was once the site of the Starlite Cafe.

***Bing's and Bank of Montreal – once Co-Op and the
New Palace Hotel***

From the north west corner of 10thstreet and 103rd avenue to the alleyway before the building that was once Kittson's Drug Store is now completely empty. The old Woolworth's building burned down in April of 2011 when it was the Wildcat Video Store. In September, 2012 the Alaska Hotel and Cafe and the Brass Scissors was ravaged by flame leaving this entire block empty until the hair dressing shop was rebuilt.

Travelling East from the Mile Zero Post on the north side, the only recognizable name on a building was Lothar Jewellers, and next to it was another empty lot. Across the street were some buildings that were very familiar; the Mile Zero Hotel and CJDC are still standing and going strong. Looking south on 9th street toward 103rd avenue is the building which was once the Government Liquor Store; above it is the Masonic hall that was the site of regular dances hosted by the Dynamics, The Volcanoes and Nighthawks bands. (Many pleasant hours spent there listening to music and dancing.) Amazingly the Dairy Queen and McLevin Brothers are still in the same place doing business as usual. The Legion's second building is still standing and has been transformed into a few smaller businesses.

Kittson's Drug Store

Lothar's Jewellers

Masonic Hall

West of the Mile Zero Post along 102nd avenue on the south side, is the Butcher Block. It was Lawrence's Meat Market and it is much larger than I remembered. I could no longer find Jack Patterson's Men's Wear; it was gobbled up by the butcher shop next door. There was no trace of Wing's Cafe but I know it was located next door to Patterson's Men's Wear.

Butcher Block – once Lawrence Meats and Jack Patterson's Mens' Wear

Walking south on 10th st from 102nd ave, I passed by another grassy vacant lot on the corner of 104th ave which once was the site of the Catholic Church. The Post Office which was across the street is now the site of the Calvin Kruk Center for the Arts.

There is a sign on the building that was Kittson's Drug Store that declares it a heritage site. I am glad to see that someone is taking an interest in preserving these iconic buildings for posterity. The corner where the Northland Theatre and the Alamo Billiard hall once stood, is now a used car parking lot for Aspol Motors.

Aspol Motors car lot – once was the Northland Theatre and the Alamo Pool Hall

I think Aspol Motors may be invincible; it has survived the blast of the 1943 explosion, the change of ownership, the pressures of competition and economic hard times. I looked inside the showroom to find that not much has changed there. I poked my head into the sales manager's office to introduce myself to Todd Logan. He is the son of my good friends Murray and Judy Logan, he was yet to be born when I left Dawson Creek. Looking across the street I could no longer see the building that was once Leach's Tire; I did see another vacant lot. Sadly, I can no longer get my favourite hamburger as Smittie's is nowhere to be found.

Some things never change; the landscape of the hills and valleys surrounding the city is pretty much the same...With the exception of the wind turbines on Bear Mountain. The creek still runs through the center of town and the sun still comes up in the east. The city structures have changed by virtue of erosion brought on by the passage of time. The face of the population has changed by the exodus of many who have gone on to live in other parts and by the influx of people drawn by wind power, coal, oil and gas industries.

The cemeteries have many headstones with the names of people who lived and died in this community. I have visited them to say hello to my family and many friends who are now a permanent part of the history of Dawson Creek.

Spring Sunrise over Dawson Creek

Time, the shadow of the footprint. At best the young footprint strives eagerly but at the same time hesitantly. It may have tasted disappointment already, sadness maybe, youthful joys innocently for sure. Nevertheless, it is a footprint in time.

Revisiting the shadows of our footprint really exposes the vulnerable act of growing up. You stand at the corner where the old high school burnt. Who but we who misted through those halls remember it? Does that absence of walls improve the formation of our lives? Does it illuminate, enhance or magnify dreams? Does it expunge the growing pains? Which prevails? Walking the old shortcuts home is never the same. The steps of an adult retracing these shadows only bares the shock of age, for time is a one way dimension bought with the price of youth. Can a generation remember the shadow of their footprint when it is soft, nearly silent, just a whisper on a breeze that is blowing by?

Dyanne Kortmeyer-Johnson

Made in the USA
Middletown, DE
20 September 2019